Events
**&** Outcomes

# THE
# SLAVE
# TRADE

Events & Outcomes

# THE
# SLAVE
# TRADE

## TOM MONAGHAN

Evans

First published in paperback in 2008
by Evans Brothers Limited
2A Portman Mansions
Chiltern Street
London W1U 6NR
UK

British Library Cataloguing in Publication Data
Monaghan, Tom
  The slave trade. - (Events and outcomes)
  1.Slave trade - Juvenile literature
  I.Title
  306.3'62

  ISBN 978 0 237 53626 8

Edited by Rachel Norridge
Designed by Neil Sayer
Maps by Tim Smith
Consultant: Dr Kevin Shillington
Printed in China by WKT Co. Ltd

# Acknowledgements

**Cover** The Bridgeman Art Library  **Background image** the art archive  **p.6** the art archive  **p.7** (top)
Mary Evans Picture Library  (bottom) Peter Newark's American Pictures  **p.8** the art archive  **p.9** The
Bridgeman Art Library  **p.11** (top) the art archive  (bottom) Mary Evans Picture Library  **p.12** (top) the
art archive  **p.14** (middle) Mary Evans Picture Library  (bottom) The Bridgeman Art Library  **p.15** Mary
Evans Picture Library  **p.16** (top) Mary Evans Picture Library  (bottom) the art archive  **p.17** (top) Mary
Evans Picture Library  (bottom) The Bridgeman Art Library  **p.18** (top) the art archive  (bottom) The
Bridgeman Art Library  **p.19** The Bridgeman Art Library  **p.20** Mary Evans Picture Library  **p.21** (top)
Mary Evans Picture Library  (bottom) The Bridgeman Art Library  **p.22** (top) Peter Newark's American
Pictures  (bottom) Topham Picturepoint  **p.23** (top) Mary Evans Picture Library  (bottom) Peter Newark's
American Pictures  **p.24** Mary Evans Picture Library  **p.25** Mary Evans Picture Library  **p.26** the art
archive  **p.27** The Bridgeman Art Library  **p.28** The Bridgeman Art Library  **p.29** Mary Evans Picture
Library  **p.30** Mary Evans Picture Library  **p.32** Mary Evans Picture Library  **p.33** Peter Newark's
American Pictures  **p.34** Peter Newark's American Pictures  **p.35** Peter Newark's American Pictures
**p.37** Mary Evans Picture Library  **p.38** Peter Newark's American Pictures  **p.39** Mary Evans Picture
Library  **p.40** The Bridgeman Art Library  **p.41** The Bridgeman Art Library  **p.42** (top) The Bridgeman
Art Library  (bottom) Mary Evans Picture Library  **p.43** the art archive  **p.44** Mary Evans Picture Library
**p.45** The Bridgeman Art Library  **p.47** (top) The Bridgeman Art Library  (bottom) The Bridgeman Art
Library  **p.48** Mary Evans Picture Library  **p.49** (top) Mary Evans Picture Library  (bottom) Mary Evans
Picture Library  **p.50** The Bridgeman Art Library  **p.51** (top) Peter Newark's American Pictures  (bottom)
the art archive  **p.52** Mary Evans Picture Library  **p.53** Mary Evans Picture Library  **p.54** the art archive
**p.55** (top) Mary Evans Picture Library  (bottom) The Bridgeman Art Library  **p.56** Mary Evans Picture
Library  **p.57** (top) Mary Evans Picture Library  (bottom) Peter Newark's American Pictures  **p.58** The
Bridgeman Art Library  **p.60** Mary Evans Picture Library  **p.61** (top) Mary Evans Picture Library  (bot-
tom) The Bridgeman Art Library  **p.62** The Bridgeman Art Library  **p.63** (top) Peter Newark's American
Pictures  (bottom) The Bridgeman Art Library  **p.64** Mary Evans Picture Library  **p.65** (top) Peter
Newark's American Pictures  (bottom) Corbis  **p.67**: (top) Topham Picturepoint  (bottom) Mary Evans
Picture Library  **p.68**: Topham Picturepoint  **p.69**: Mary Evans Picture Library  **p.70**: Topham Picturepoint
**p.71**: Topham Picturepoint  **p.72**: Mary Evans Picture Library

# CONTENTS

# THE ORIGINS OF SLAVERY

This basalt stone tablet, dating from nearly 4,000 years ago, is inscribed with Hammurabi, the King of Babylon's code of law. Among its 300 laws, the code states that helping a slave to escape was to be punished by a death sentence; slaves who escaped but were recaptured could be executed.

## Slavery in the Ancient World

Slavery is the enforced servitude of people to another person or group. A slave is regarded as someone's property through birth, purchase or capture. As a social and economic institution, slavery appears to have originated when humans abandoned hunting and gathering in favour of subsistence farming. Among early civilisations, references to slavery are recorded in the Babylonian code of Hammurabi, and in the Bible. Forms of slavery were known in ancient China, and slave labour was a fact of life in ancient Greece and Rome, where slaves worked on large estates and met the demand for domestic servants in towns and cities. Often, slaves were prisoners of war, the children of slave parents, children sold into slavery by free parents, or criminals condemned to servitude.

## Slavery in Asia and Africa

Numerous types of servitude developed throughout the world to serve a range of purposes, from solving a chronic labour shortage to serving as victims of ritual sacrifice. As well as being employed as agricultural labourers and servants, some slaves were able to exercise considerable power as stewards who managed large estates in China. Some slaves were captured as young boys in southern Europe, and forcibly converted to Islam, before being given a rigorous military training by their African or Middle Eastern owners. These warriors were able to achieve high rank in the armies of some Islamic countries, although female slaves were more highly prized than males in most parts of Africa and the Middle East, since they often served as wives and concubines. In Africa, a trans-Saharan trade in captives for sale into slavery existed before, during and after the period of the transatlantic slave trade.

## Slavery in Europe

Following the decline of the Roman Empire in the west, a prominent feature of European society was the large

Russian serfs were not given their freedom until the second half of the nineteenth century, like so many slaves in the New World. Were the serfs' lives so very different from the lives of slaves in the Americas?

number of agricultural slaves known as serfs. These slaves were bound by law to the land where they worked. Serfdom in various forms was a common form of agricultural labour and persisted until at least the nineteenth century in some parts of Europe. In areas of France, elements of serfdom survived until the French Revolution at the end of the eighteenth century when nobles renounced their feudal rights. Another form of forced labour or servitude in modern Europe was the custom of young apprentices or servants signing a contract that bound them to a master for a number of years in return for food and shelter and, possibly, learning a trade.

## Slavery in the New World

Following the defeat of the Moors in Spain and Portugal in the fifteenth century, captured Muslims were enslaved by the victorious Christians. Soon, these prisoners of war were joined by slaves imported from Africa. A regular trade in slaves was established between the Guinea coast of Africa and the Iberian peninsular. Colonists cultivating sugar cane on Atlantic islands, such as Madeira and the Canaries, relied on a mixture of slave and free labour. In the sixteenth century, African slaves were transported to colonies in the Americas, marking the beginning of a transatlantic slave trade that would transform the history of West Africa, and play a huge part in the social and economic development of Western Europe and the Americas.

African captives landing at Jamestown, Virginia, in 1619.

PART I: DEVELOPMENT OF THE
TRANSATLANTIC SLAVE TRADE

# EUROPE AND THE
# SLAVE TRADE

## New World Colonies

The transatlantic slave trade developed in the sixteenth century as European states established colonies in South and Central America. In the last decade of the fifteenth century, following the discoveries of Christopher Columbus on his expeditions to the New World, the Spanish established colonies in the eastern half of Haiti, Cuba, other islands in the Caribbean and in what is known as South America. In 1500, Portugal took possession of Brazil, and it was to become their largest and most important colony in the Americas.

Colonisation continued early in the seventeenth century with the English taking over Barbados, Jamaica and several other Caribbean islands, while the French settled in Guadaloupe and Martinique. In order to exploit the economic potential of these colonies, the European colonial powers needed an extensive supply of labour. For example, where conditions were favourable, the Spanish and Portuguese had started to grow sugar cane to be processed and shipped back to Europe.

The harvesting, and processing of sugar cane to produce sugar in its many forms became the focus of economic life on many Caribbean islands, such as Antigua.

Plantations were established in Brazil, Mexico, Paraguay, the Pacific coast of South America and islands in the Caribbean. They had also discovered that crops such as rice, citrus fruits, olives and tobacco grew well in these new colonies. Native inhabitants were pressed into service as forced labour, but many died of overwork, disease and hunger, or simply ran off into the forests. Free labour from Europe chose to live in urban areas where they were employed as craftsmen and artisans, or took to self-employment in agriculture because fertile land was abundant. The Spanish and Portuguese therefore decided to import slave labour from the Atlantic islands and mainland Africa to work on sugar plantations, coffee and cocoa estates, or in gold and diamond mines.

## European Consumers

Population growth and economic change had led to improved standards of living in European towns and cities. This increased consumer demand for plantation produce such as sugar, tobacco, coffee and cocoa. In response, colonists in the Americas enlarged their estates and purchased slave labour from Africa to increase the production of crops that commanded a high price from European traders. Therefore, growing consumer demand for colonial produce in European markets encouraged colonists to purchase more slaves to meet that demand.

The *Southall* frigate was one of many European vessels trading on the coast of West Africa in the seventeenth century. Its crew would have found African traders eager to obtain European goods in exchange for captives.

The Spanish and Portuguese shipped huge numbers of African slaves across the Atlantic to work in colonies such as Cuba and Brazil. Next, the Dutch took advantage of their enormous banking and shipping resources to become financiers of the burgeoning slave trade. They supplied many of the slave ships required to transport tens of thousands of Africans to servitude in the New World.

## The French Colonies

The expansion of output in the French colonies did not occur until the last quarter of the eighteenth century, with the most dramatic development taking place in the colony of Saint-Domingue. From 1760, this French colony's sugar production expanded dramatically, and the colonists set about increasing their production of coffee and cotton by taking advantage of the terrain and soil of their island. The result of this expansion in plantation production was a huge increase in the number of slaves employed in the colony, and the proportion of African-born slaves within the total population of Saint-Domingue was greater than that of any other large colony in the Americas.

# Triangular Trade

European governments were attracted to the economic benefits of possessing colonies in the New World, and sought to exploit the commercial advantages of using slave labour. Slavery and the trade in slaves proved to be major factors in the economic development of Europe's colonial powers. A lucrative long-distance transatlantic slave trade developed as a complex network of commercial enterprises. Contemporaries, however, identified a triangular trade. First, European goods such as alcohol, firearms and textiles were shipped from Europe to be traded for slaves in West Africa. Second, the slaves would then be shipped to South America or the Caribbean where they would be traded for staples such as sugar, rice, and later, raw cotton. Third, these products of the New World colonies were exported to Europe and sold for large profits. In reality, the trade was much more complex than this simple description. For example, in the eighteenth century, two out of every five slave ships sailed to and from ports in the Americas.

A map showing the eighteenth-century triangular transatlantic trade.

## The Extent of the Trade

During the eighteenth century, European merchants controlled the transatlantic slave trade along a 1,000-mile stretch of the West African coast. At least ten million African captives were transported across the Atlantic between 1500 and the end of the nineteenth century. By the end of the eighteenth century, two African captives had crossed the Atlantic for every European colonist who had sailed to the New World. Half of those Africans were transported in the eighteenth century, and most were carried on Portuguese, British or French vessels, with assistance from Spanish, Dutch, Danish and Swedish ships. A significant proportion of the Portuguese and British

In the late seventeenth century, European slave traders could spend months sailing up and down the African coast. They would row ashore at regular intervals to meet chiefs and traders who could supply them with captives to fill their holds before they set off on the Middle Passage.

comme les Negres ram<u>ent</u> de bout

Commerce

Documents, like this list of slaves exported from Cameroon at the end of the eighteenth century, are often the only clue to the ethnic origin of the millions of captives who were transported to the New World.

ships sailed from colonies in the Americas. Some British slave traders operated out of ports in New England and Barbados. They supplied colonies in the Caribbean and on the mainland of North and South America, while Portuguese traders sailed from Bahia in Brazil and supplied their own colonies. In total, Brazil and the Caribbean bought 90 per cent of the African captives who survived the journey, known as the 'Middle Passage', from West Africa to the West Indies.

During the eighteenth century, slaves accounted for about 70 per cent of the total population of the Caribbean region, and on those European colonies where sugar cane was the main crop, the slave population could account for nearly 90 per cent of the total population. The size of the slave population in Europe's American colonies reached its peak at the end of the eighteenth century, although the number of slaves in the former European colonies of Brazil and the United States of America continued to grow until the 1840s and 1850s, respectively.

Slave caravans were crossing North Africa long before the Europeans took an interest in the trade. European slave traders were able to take advantage of existing trade routes and African merchants' contacts and expertise.

# The Effects in Africa

In the years before the transatlantic slave trade developed, the Europeans had bought African slaves who had been transported by slave traders across the Sahara region to North Africa. As the number of captives being transported across the Atlantic Ocean grew, trade between Africans and Europeans stimulated change and growth in the economy of West Africa.

African farming was adapted to grow crops used to provision the slave ships. The areas that supplied agricultural produce for the transatlantic trade were not always the same as those that supplied slaves. Captives were taken from almost the whole area of West Africa, but crops were supplied from areas with reliable transport links to the trading stations on the coast. The reason for this was the high cost of transport in West Africa. Marching captives to the coast presented few problems, but agricultural produce had to be transported, either by water or on porters' heads. Since the price of a single captive was roughly equivalent to that of a ton of palm oil (which would require about 60 porters to transport it any distance), it was not profitable to produce palm oil or any other agricultural produce for export unless it was grown close to the coast or a navigable river.

Captives were transported long distances to reach the markets and trading centres on the west coast of Africa.

# Slave Trading Centres in Africa

On the coast of West Africa, as many as 75 per cent of African captives embarked from Luanda, the Zaire or Congo River, the Niger Delta, and the Bight of Benin. Coastal states developed transport and trading networks that were able to supply small trading centres or larger stone trading forts with captives from the interior. European slave traders expected supplies to be regular and reliable. At some trading sites, African merchants developed road and river networks from the interior to the coast. One British slave trader, Thomas Clarkson, described in 1789 how he accompanied African traders as their fleet of canoes,

*called at villages as we passed, and purchased our slaves fairly; but in the night they made several excursions on the banks of the river ... broke into the villages ... and seized men, women and children.*

Over time, the focus of the slave trade moved south, and West Central Africa was the centre of the trade in its final decades. When the British attempted to enforce a ban on the transatlantic slave trade in the nineteenth century, traders south of the equator continued to supply Brazil and Cuba from Angola and Mozambique. As colonies developed and required more forced labour, some regions of Africa supplied the bulk of slaves shipped to particular colonies.

The Portuguese colony of Brazil received most of its slaves from Angola and the Bight of Benin, also known as the Slave Coast. The French colony of Saint-Domingue took a large proportion of its captives from the Bight of Benin, too. The British colonies were supplied with captives from a wide range of regions, but the Bight of Biafra, the Gold Coast and Angola were the United Kingdom's main sources of slaves in the second half of the eighteenth century. The island of Cuba was unique in that the Spanish government allowed the colony to receive slave shipments from most European merchants and, as a result, no single African region supplied more than one-third of Cuba's slaves.

Key

- British
- French
- Spanish
- Portuguese

0 — 1000 miles
0 — 1500 km

A map of West Africa, showing the location of the chief slave-trading regions.

# European Trade with Africa

European traders tried to cheat the Africans at every turn. Alcohol was diluted with water, gunpowder barrels had false bottoms, and pieces were cut out of rolls of cloth. Chiefs and kings stopped ruling by traditional laws and customs, and became greedy tyrants, taking advice from the slave traders' ruthless European agents. In the sixteenth century, King Affonso of the Congo complained to the Portuguese that,

The vast majority of African children who were abducted by raiders would be unable to trace their parents or return to their home villages.

*so great is the corruption and lawlessness that our country is being completely depopulated.*

Tribal wars became more common, encouraged by the profits that could be made from the slave trade. Law and justice were corrupted as more and more crimes, no matter how small, were punished by enslavement. Thousands of villages were progressively deserted as a result of wars or raids to capture slaves.

# Africans Supply Slaves

Some African states which had enslaved captives for many years, enslaved yet more people when the transatlantic slave trade developed. From the late seventeenth century, Ashanti (Asante) traded slaves and captives for European goods, such as cloth, alcohol and guns. It used these resources to make itself more powerful, and to start wars against its neighbours to acquire more captives. Another African kingdom that took advantage of the transatlantic slave trade was Dahomey. In the eighteenth century, the kings of Dahomey organised

This image of the King of Dahomey gives us some idea of the power and prestige of those African rulers who profited from the trade in African captives.

raids into neighbouring lands largely to capture prisoners to sell on to European traders. On a smaller scale, other kingdoms took part in the slave trade, venturing far inland to take captives to sell on to Europeans. In these coastal areas, native crafts died out, unable to compete with cheap European goods mass produced in factories.

## The Profits of Slave Labour

The transatlantic trade in human cargo, and the crops that slave labour produced, financed the building of new harbours and the construction of new shipyards in the British Isles. In turn, this led to increased orders for British factories producing goods for export to Africa and the American colonies. In the second half of the eighteenth century, Britain's major seaports made huge profits from transatlantic trade.

Slaves produced about 75 per cent of the total value of exports from the Americas traded in the Atlantic area in the seventeenth and eighteenth centuries. By the end of the eighteenth century, British industries producing for export markets that included the Americas were growing faster than those producing mainly for the domestic market. Liverpool merchants sent a petition to Parliament in 1788 that claimed that abolition of the slave trade would,

 *ruin the property of the English merchants in the West Indies, diminish the public revenue and impair (weaken) the maritime strength of Great Britain.*

## Race Relations

Ethnic and religious differences between the European slave owners and their African slaves helped to legitimise master–slave relationships, and distinguish between those who could be forcibly enslaved and those who could not. Modern European slavery in the colonial era was characterised by its ethnic composition. Most slaves were African by birth, or the descendants of Africans who had been transported to European colonies in North and South America. Most slave owners were Europeans or their descendants.

Diverse conditions and traditions fostered variations between societies in the European colonies, both in terms of slavery and race relations, but it is true to say that slavery in Europe's American colonies was predicated on an unequal relationship between Europeans and non-Europeans. This inequality has had repercussions for race relations in the Atlantic world ever since.

In the eighteenth century, the ownership of slaves in Britain's American colonies provided a large labour force on plantations, and was a measure of wealth and prestige.

# European Civilisation and Slavery

From ancient times, European states had exploited slave labour. Ancient attitudes towards Europeans who were enslaved were similar to those faced by African captives in the modern era. The Greek soldier Xenophon wrote a manual for slave owners, giving advice on how to select suitable slaves for employment on a large estate. In particular, he emphasised the qualities of intelligence, energy, loyalty and experience required by any slave in a position of responsibility.

Xenophon's book on how to handle slaves reminds us that early Europeans took slavery for granted.

The philosopher Plato, writing 2,500 years ago, believed that Greeks should not be enslaved by Greeks, but he did not conclude that slavery was unjust. Instead, he wrote that slavery should be restricted to foreigners or 'barbarians', and that the status of slave could be inherited from parents. At that stage in European civilisation, the idea had developed that those who were enslaved were inferior to their owners. The philosopher Aristotle, who was a pupil of Plato, wrote that:

*From the hour of their birth some are marked out for subjection, others for rule.*

The brutal treatment of captives and the enslavement of prisoners came together in the use of slave gladiators in the arenas of the Roman Empire.

Aristotle went so far as to suggest that it was the duty of superior Greeks to enslave inferior barbarians, in order that both groups could fulfil their true functions, to their mutual benefit.

# Ancient Rome

The Roman Empire swallowed up most of southern and western Europe, and most of North Africa. Slaves were imperial victims whose lives were held cheap by ruthless rulers who enjoyed absolute power over their imperial conquests. For centuries, the citizens of the Roman Empire demanded the deaths of thousands of slave gladiators each year for their entertainment, and tolerated the branding, burning, beating and mutilation of slaves by owners who believed that these humans were property, not people with civil rights. Roman ideas about government and society continued to influence European civilisation when the transatlantic slave trade developed.

An artist's impression of Peruvians from Lima, drawn about 1700. Three centuries later, archaeologists are still uncovering evidence of the achievements of the civilisations that inhabited the Americas before the arrival of Europeans in the fifteenth and sixteenth centuries.

# Exploration and Oppression

The Portuguese and Spanish explorers who set sail for the New World across the Atlantic in the wake of Columbus in the 1490s, took for granted their right to enslave enemies and exploit forced labour. Mistakenly believing that they were exploring the Indies in South-East Asia, the explorers had called the people who lived on these islands 'Indians'. A more serious error was the failure of these explorers to appreciate the differences between their own European culture and beliefs, and those of the many peoples whom they encountered. The simple technology, hospitality and generosity of so many indigenous peoples were mistaken for signs of weakness, and the superiority of European civilisation was assumed at all times. Columbus described the inhabitants of the island that he named Hispaniola as being kind, peaceful and generous, but he noted in his journal that:

*With fifty men they could all be subjected and made to do all that I wished.*

# European Violence

Contact between Europe and the New World led to death and misery on a huge scale. Within fifty years of Columbus setting foot on the island, it is estimated that the indigenous population of Hispaniola fell from approximately 300,000 to less than 1,000, due to disease, war and the mistreatment of captives. From the outset, servitude in the Americas would be characterised by cruelty and violence towards non-Europeans. By 1600, nearly one million African captives had been transported across the Atlantic. Most of these victims would meet a fate similar to that of the peoples whom they were being used to replace as forced labour. The development of Europe's transatlantic trade demanded a high price of captives who were exploited by traders who paid scant respect to the humanity of their victims.

Plantation records, government files, colonists' diaries and letters, and the accounts left by freed men and women describe the brutality that slave ownership encouraged and condoned.

# THE MIDDLE PASSAGE

This image of two merchants on an island off Senegal is a reminder of how European slave traders developed close links with the Africans who supplied captives for the Middle Passage.

Two iron slave collars from around 1790. Archaeologists have found collars and chains small enough to fit children, or small adults.

## Coastal Trade

In Africa, most of the trade in captives was carried out at markets in the small trading factories or larger stone forts along the Atlantic coast. Where there were no proper harbour facilities, slave ships would sail up and down the coast collecting batches of captives who had been ferried to the ships in small boats and canoes. Ships' captains had to inspect the captives to assess whether or not they would survive the voyage and make a good price in the slave markets in the New World. Some captains could spend four or five months plying their trade along the African coast until they had enough slaves to fill their holds.

## The Middle Passage

The death rate among sailors involved in trade with Africa was very high. Since a significant proportion of the crew was likely to die from disease before they reached the Americas, crew levels could fall to dangerous levels. Slave ship captains had to be prepared to face storms and slave rebellions during what was known as the 'Middle Passage', and they needed as large a crew as possible to reach the slave markets on the other side of the Atlantic Ocean.

Adult females made up about 25 per cent of the African captives who were forced into slavery in the Americas. For much of the eighteenth century, this ratio was largely determined by African supply conditions. Most captives were prisoners of war who were predominately male – female slaves were in much higher demand than males in Africa's domestic slave trade.

Children of both sexes made up roughly ten per cent of the slaves carried on the Middle Passage. Their numbers declined rapidly due to physical and sexual abuse aboard the vessels, and the ravages of smallpox, measles and other diseases that contributed to the high mortality rate among the younger captives. As there were so few female slaves in relation to males, the slave populations in most European colonies in the New World failed to reproduce their numbers.

Slave vessels setting sail on the Middle Passage from West African trading centres on the Gambia, Senegal and Sierra Leone rivers could take four to six weeks to complete the voyage. The passage could take several months from regions closer to the equator such as the Bight of Benin. Early in the history of the transatlantic slave trade, almost twenty per cent of African captives died during the Middle Passage. By the late eighteenth century, less than ten per cent of slaves died crossing the Atlantic, mainly due to improvements in hygiene and sanitation aboard ships.

## Bills of Exchange

Slave ship captains and colonial merchants sold slaves to plantation owners in return for what were known as bills of exchange. These bills could be exchanged for return cargoes of plantation produce, but most slave vessels were not large enough to transport more than a fraction of the colonies' produce back to Europe. Instead, most colonial produce was carried on larger vessels known to the British as 'West Indiamen'. The smaller slave-carrying vessels did not play a significant part in the final leg of the triangular trade.

A Dutch ship landing captives at Jamestown in 1619. Most African captives were initially landed in the Caribbean and South America in the seventeenth and eighteenth centuries. Captives were carried in ships from most major European trading nations.

## Slave Ships

Slave ships were small by modern standards, although they grew in size between the seventeenth and nineteenth centuries, from about 100 to 300 tons. Slave ships were rigged for speed and most carried between 200 and 300 captives. Contemporary diagrams of slave ships show how the captives were stacked below decks for the voyage. Often there were two levels, one above the other, on either side of the ship. Adult male captives had their right foot shackled to the left foot of the person on their right, and their left foot shackled to the right foot of the person on their left. The human cargo had little or no head room, making it impossible for them to sit up. Because they were chained, they found it difficult to change position. A doctor in 1790 noted that on overcrowded ships the captives,

*complained of heat and want of air. Confinement in this situation was so injurious that he has known them to go down apparently in good health at night and found dead in the morning.*

Women and children were not chained as a rule, but were liable to face physical and sexual abuse from sailors throughout the voyage.

Each day, when the weather permitted, some captives were taken on deck to exercise. Exercise, or 'dancing', was thought to prevent outbreaks of disease among the captives. When the sea was rough or the weather was inclement, the captives were kept below deck for long periods, and the sick and healthy, living and dead or dying, remained manacled together for days on end. Despite most ships carrying a medical assistant or doctor, outbreaks of dysentery were common due to the filthy conditions and lack of clean drinking water.

## Captive Resistance

Many African captives on the Middle Passage committed suicide. Some captives took the opportunity when exercising above deck to jump overboard and drown. Some appeared to lose the will to live and died from

Deck plans for the slave ship *Brookes* which sailed out of Liverpool, England, at the end of the eighteenth century. Each male captive was allowed less than 1.8m by 40cm of room, so that the vessel could pack in 450 slaves.

what was called 'fixed melancholy'. These captives would refuse to eat, and to discourage this form of resistance crews would beat these captives or torture them with thumbscrews. If this did not work, sailors would force-feed the captives by opening their jaws and forcing food into their mouths. Crews were known to use chisels to break the teeth of captives who resisted being force-fed. The slave traders were worried that if one captive refused to eat, others would follow suit and a large number of valuable Africans would die.

In fair weather, small groups of captives were brought up onto the main deck to dance during the voyage. This kept them fit and healthy, so they would fetch a good price when they reached the slave markets in the Americas.

## Slave Rebellions

Europeans were always on guard against captives attempting to take control of the ship by killing the crew. One slave trader, John Newton, noted in his journal in 1753 that:

 *I was at first continually alarmed with the slaves' almost desperate attempts to make attacks upon us.*

Rebellions were most likely to occur when ships were off the African coast, before they set sail across the Atlantic. Most uprisings were put down ruthlessly by the European crews, but there were a few occasions when captives took control of the vessel on which they had been held captive. In 1742, the British vessel *Mary* was driven ashore on the River Gambia by the local people, and the captives on board seized the opportunity to kill most of the crew before escaping. However, the success of these captives was the exception rather than the rule.

A contemporary illustration showing the death of Captain Ferrer of the *Amistad*, when the captives seized control of the ship. The future of the captives aboard the *Amistad* led to a legal battle in the USA courts between the ship's owners and abolitionists.

The sale of African captives could take place aboard the slave ship, on a beach, or in a large sea port. This seventeenth-century Dutch auction of African slaves took place ashore in New Amsterdam (later New York).

# Preparations For Sale

Having completed the voyage across the Atlantic, slave traders were determined to present their African captives to potential purchasers in the best possible condition. The captives who had survived the voyage were washed and fed for several days. Males were shaved and older captives had their grey hair dyed to make it more difficult to guess their age. Often, their skin was rubbed with palm oil to give their bodies a healthy sheen. Older or less healthy individuals might not attract any bids from colonists or their agents. They could be taken on to other islands where they could be put up for sale until they attracted a buyer, but sometimes these 'refuse' slaves were left to die of neglect, unattended at the quayside of the port where they had disembarked.

This branding iron was used to mark and identify slaves on arrival.

# Slave Sales

The captives could be sold aboard the ship, soon after it arrived, or at a public auction ashore. In some ports, the captains of slave ships handed their human cargo over to agents for the vessels' owners. These agents inspected the captives as if they were livestock, checking limbs and teeth for defects, before advertising the place and time of the slave sale. Captives would be listed for sale by sex, approximate age and sometimes provenance or geographic origin, if known.

In Spanish and Portuguese colonies, newly-arrived slaves would be branded with a red hot iron to indicate that they had been imported legally.

In the Caribbean, captives were often sold through a 'scramble' when prospective purchasers and their associates ran forward and claimed those captives whom they wanted to buy at an agreed price. Despite attempts to present new arrivals as fit and healthy, many colonists avoided buying captives who had just completed the Middle Passage since they could be carrying infectious diseases that threatened the existing slave population. Some colonists were not prepared to train recently arrived captives, who had to be acclimatised to their new environment and taught the skills of plantation labourers. Although some colonists were prepared to wait until newly-purchased slaves had recovered from the effects of the Atlantic crossing, many put new arrivals to work at once, especially if they were purchased at harvest time when labour was in short supply.

Many African captives were bought in Barbados and the Leeward Islands by slave traders who shipped them to the North American mainland, where they were sold either to colonists, or to other traders who sold them on to slave owners in the interior of the colonies. Charleston in South Carolina was the main port of direct entry for slaves in North America during the eighteenth century. Here, ships carrying captives had to wait outside the port at Sullivan Island for ten days. If the slaves aboard any ship turned out to be suffering from smallpox, the ship would be quarantined for at least four weeks.

When they were sold, captives would be separated from their fellow victims who had accompanied them on the Middle Passage, and they would be given a European name in place of their African name.

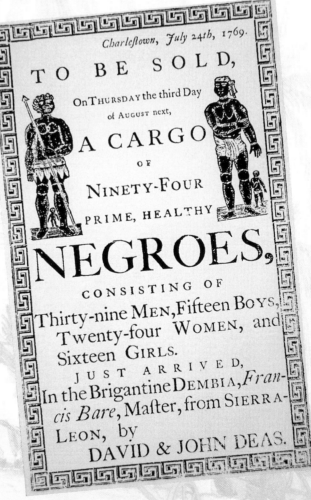

A poster advertising a slave auction of captives from Sierra Leone in Charleston, South Carolina, 1769.

# The European Enlightenment

The term 'Enlightenment' refers to the changes in attitudes and beliefs that began in Europe around 300 years ago. European scientists, philosophers and political commentators in the eighteenth century, many known as *philosophes*, were united in the belief that rational, critical study and analysis should be applied in all matters. Many criticised political, social and economic practices that appeared to be irrational, such as superstitious religion or tyrannical rulers. They argued that the rational or reasoned foundation of government should be the welfare or well-being of the governed, who had 'natural rights' such as the right to fight against tyranny. These ideas developed at a time when Europeans were reaping the benefits of employing millions of slaves in the Americas. Rousseau, in his *Social Contract* (1762), wrote that:

*Man was born free, but everywhere he is in chains.*

# Revolutionary Ideals

At the time of the American Revolution, slavery and the slave trade remained key elements of economic prosperity in a large number of the colonies, united in their fight against British rule. In their Declaration of Independence, the American colonists included the enlightened phrase:

*All men are created equal.*

Thomas Jefferson (1743–1826), third president of the USA under the present constitution, was a Founding Father of the USA and a slave owner.

In the draft of this Declaration, Thomas Jefferson, a slave owner, had condemned the slave trade. However, it is clear that he believed that Africans were inferior beings to Europeans, and he was not prepared to give up his property or lose political influence through active opposition to slavery. The leaders of the American Revolution who were influenced by the ideas of the eighteenth-century Enlightenment were not social revolutionaries. When the federal constitution of the United States was drafted in 1787, the legal status of slavery in the Southern states, where about 90 per cent of American slaves lived, was strengthened.

In the 1790s, the French revolutionaries set out the principles of their revolution in a Declaration of the Rights of Man and of the Citizen that stated:

 *Men are born free and remain free and equal in their rights.*

Despite the lofty ideals of the Enlightenment, political intrigue and economic self-interest meant that slavery and the slave trade would remain facts of life for too many people in the French empire. In 1794, the French abolished slavery in their colonies, and accepted all colonial males as full citizens, only for Napoleon Bonaparte to restore colonial slavery in 1802.

## Humanitarian Ideals

Influenced by the ideals of the Enlightenment, some Europeans embarked on crusades against colonial slavery rather than against other forms of servitude and forced labour closer to home. From the beginning, campaigns against slavery exhibited a form of paternalism towards Africans and their descendants in European colonies. This approach was encouraged by real or imagined images of exotic, but apparently primitive, societies and cultures in Africa and the Americas, which gave some credibility to a simplistic moral crusade on behalf of Africans. Even those who opposed slavery were guilty of assuming that slaves were somehow inferior to free Europeans.

A public execution at Tyburn in London. A death sentence was common for most serious, as well as many less serious, crimes in eighteenth- and nineteenth-century Europe. How far did humanitarian ideals really extend at this time?

# CHAPTER THREE

# SLAVE LIFE IN THE AMERICAS

## Slave Imports

More than 90 per cent of the slaves who were transported across the Atlantic were imported by European colonies on the South American mainland, or on the Caribbean islands. Conditions in these colonies were so harsh that slave deaths exceeded slave births. Climate, tropical diseases and exhausting labour on sugar plantations contributed to the failure of the slave populations in these colonies to achieve natural population growth. Slave owners continued to import large numbers of African slaves until the trade was abolished. Despite the existence of an illegal slave trade well into the nineteenth century, the slave population continued to decline.

## The Sugar Trade

This illustration of sugar manufacture in the Antilles in 1726 is evidence of the labour-intensive production methods that were necessary to produce sugar that could be exported to Europe.

Several European states took advantage of the trading opportunities made possible by establishing colonies in the Americas. By the middle of the eighteenth century, most European colonies in the region were committed to exporting sugar. Five British islands in the Caribbean produced cotton, timber, fish, livestock and salt, but fourteen British colonies concentrated on sugar production. By 1789, the French island of Saint-Domingue was the single largest sugar-producing colony in the Americas. The Dutch colony of Suriname on the mainland of South America imported African slaves to work on its plantations, and around one quarter of the population of the Danish island of Saint Thomas were slaves employed on sugar plantations. The Swedish colony of Saint Barthelemy was an exception in that its slaves were restricted to working as domestic servants or as farm labourers producing food for consumption on the island.

On sugar plantations, slaves worked under the gang system and were assigned tasks and roles according to colour of skin, place of birth, gender, state of health, age and skills. Slaves who were considered by their European owners to have lighter skins, and had been born in the Americas, were preferred for domestic service. Male and female slaves worked in the fields and there was little or no difference in the types of field work carried out by either sex. Men and women were expected to tackle the most arduous tasks in the fields and sugar factories. An eighteenth-century Swiss visitor to Saint-Domingue described how he saw,

Slaves planting sugar canes in Antigua in 1823. How would the working day of a plantation slave differ from the experience of a free labourer employed in similar activities?

*about a hundred men and women of different ages, all occupied in digging ditches in a cane-field, the majority of them naked or covered in rags.*

# Field Labour on Plantations

At harvest time, slaves on sugar plantations had to work shifts of eighteen to twenty-four hours for five or six months at a time, since the sugar cane had to be processed without interruption. Field labour on sugar plantations was divided into three gangs. The first gang consisted of the fittest and healthiest slaves of both sexes who were experts in preparing the soil for cultivation, digging cane holes, planting and manuring the canes, burning and cutting the sugar cane at harvest time, and performing manual labour in the sugar mills. They worked under the supervision of European overseers and male slave-drivers.

The second gang was supervised by a male slave-driver and was made up of less fit males and females, pregnant or nursing females and slaves recently arrived from Africa. They performed a variety of less physically demanding tasks, including weeding crops, carrying manure to the cane fields and feeding crushed cane stalks into the sugar factory furnaces. The third gang consisted of children up to the age of twelve or thirteen who were supervised by a mature female slave, and this gang looked after the plantation's livestock.

Slaves employed in processing sugar cane developed considerable expertise and a range of skills that were valued by their owners. However, paying wages to an army of workers would have made these methods uneconomic.

28

On many Caribbean islands, and to a lesser extent in Brazil, a significant number of slaves were able to achieve a level of economic independence by cultivating crops on plots of land granted by their masters. These slaves could sell their surplus and acquire their own property and possessions.

## Slave Emancipation

Despite attempts to bring the transatlantic slave trade to an end, African captives continued to be transported to the Americas for much of the nineteenth century, until slavery was abolished throughout South America and the Caribbean. A revolution in Saint-Domingue between 1791 and 1804 won independence for the French colony, and freed its slaves. The colony's slaves had marched to the words of a song that stated:

*Better to die than go on being a slave.*

Former slaves celebrating their emancipation in Barbados, August 1834. Similar scenes were repeated throughout the Americas in the nineteenth century by millions of freed labourers.

Sweden had handed back its only Caribbean colony to the French, long before slavery was abolished in the British Empire in 1834. All slaves were freed in the French and Danish colonies by 1848, and the Dutch abolished slavery in their colonies in 1863. Slavery came to an end in the Spanish Caribbean between 1870 and 1886, but Brazilian slaves were not emancipated until 1888.

Slavery remained profitable and therefore viable in both Brazil and Cuba until the 1870s, despite attempts by the Portuguese and Spanish governments to end the use of forced labour in both colonies. In the end, it would be political and technological change that would emancipate these slaves. In the case of Cuba, a more liberal regime in Spain and pro-independence rebels in the colony both declared their support for emancipation. Once the powerful plantation owners had built large, modern sugar mills, served by a network of railway lines, Cuban slaves were free to become wage labourers, employed on a seasonal basis. Direct action by free citizens, allied to the introduction of more efficient machinery in sugar mills, ended slavery in Brazil in the late 1880s.

As forced labour, most slaves employed in the fields had to be compelled to work by their owners and drivers. Beatings and whippings, or the threat of them, were a fact of life for most field hands.

## Slavery in North America

Farmers in the North American colonies discovered that huge profits could be made from growing and exporting crops such as tobacco and rice to Europe. Where fertile land was plentiful, but labour was in short supply, the most practical solution was the use of forced or slave labour. Some of the indigenous inhabitants of the colonies had been enslaved, but several factors prevented the development of large-scale slavery in this population, including the fact that so many of them had died in epidemics that swept through local communities with no immunity to diseases such as smallpox and measles. Also, the European colonists preferred to kill or drive away these people, rather than consider the employment of local inhabitants as agricultural labour.

## From Indenture to Slavery

In the first half of the seventeenth century, the solution to the colonists' labour shortage was the employment of indentured or bond servants. Indentured servitude meant that Europeans unable to afford to pay for their own passage to the American colonies could sell their labour to colonists for an agreed number of years, in exchange for their transportation to America. Although criminals were transported to the American colonies, most bond servants were young males from poor backgrounds, attempting to escape from poverty, hunger, unemployment or military service. Children often served seven or more years, but most adults served four or five years of indentured service. Discipline could be brutal and the corporal punishment of runaways was a common practice.

From 1650 to 1700, although the free population of some colonies doubled or tripled, the number of indentured servants did not keep pace with the demand for farm labour. In Europe, higher wages and improved employment opportunities at home meant that fewer people were attracted to indentured servitude in North America. Colonial landowners who were unable to obtain a constant supply of European servants decided to use African slaves instead. Unlike indentured servitude, slavery was for life, and it was common for female slaves to pass their status on to their children, even if a child's father was a European. The African American writer W. E. B. DuBois wrote that:

 *We cannot forget that America was built on Africa ... America became through African labour the centre of the sugar empire and the cotton kingdom.*

## American-born Slaves

Out of the ten to eleven million Africans who crossed the Atlantic on the Middle Passage, only six per cent of that total were taken to the British colonies in North America. In the eighteenth century, and in sharp contrast to the Caribbean and South America, the slave population of North America experienced a natural population growth. By the 1760s, the number of American-born slaves in the colonies overtook the number of African-born slaves. After the transatlantic slave trade ended in 1808, the slave population of the United States of America more than tripled by 1860, from 1.2 million to 4 million, and only a tiny proportion of these slaves were African-born. The fact that so many slaves in North America had been born in the colonies meant that relations between free people and the slave population were profoundly different from those in the rest of the New World.

## Slavery Declines in the North

Slaves had never formed a significant proportion of the population in the Northern colonies. Climate and soil conditions meant that plantation farming and the need for a large labour force did not develop in those colonies. In addition, religious and political principles in the Northern states meant that many people were uneasy at the existence of slavery in their communities. The growth of industry and urban communities in the North led to the development of a working class that was hostile to competition from slave labour. It was felt that slave labour would lead to lower wages and less favourable working conditions. As a result, anti-slavery campaigners found it relatively easy to rid the Northern states of slavery.

## Slavery Develops in the South

The invention of Whitney's cotton gin, or engine, in the 1790s encouraged the rapid growth of cotton production in the Deep South of the USA. How different would the social and economic development of the Southern states have been without Whitney's invention?

Meanwhile, slavery had become entrenched in the South. The booming market in cotton was largely responsible for this development. To meet the growing demand for cotton fibre in British textile factories, plantation owners had needed to find a more efficient method of separating cotton seeds from their fibre. In the 1790s, Eli Whitney designed a machine that,

*would clear the cotton with expedition (speed).*

A horse-powered gin could seed fifty times as much cotton as before, in the same amount of time.

When cotton became the USA's main agricultural export in the first half of the nineteenth century, farmers discovered that large profits could be made from growing cotton on relatively small holdings, as well as larger plantations. This meant that most American slaves did not live on huge estates. In 1860, less than three per cent of slave owners in the South owned more than 50 slaves, and no more than one out of every thousand slave owners possessed more than 200 slaves. The larger plantations concentrated on growing sugar and rice. Cotton growers tended to live on their land, and personally supervised the work of their slaves. Only on larger plantations would professional overseers be employed to carry out the instructions of their employers, usually under the watchful eyes of a resident owner.

African slaves who worked on large Southern sugar plantations did so under the watchful eye of an overseer.

## Life for Southern Slaves

The treatment and condition of slaves in the Southern states varied in relation to location, the crop grown, the size of farm or plantation and the attitude of the slave owner. On the other hand, it is possible to draw some general conclusions about slavery in the USA. Slavery was overwhelmingly based on agriculture. Most slaves were employed in the production of cotton, rice, tobacco, hemp, wheat, maize and sugar. Most lived on plantations and farms with between 15 and 50 slaves. Slaves had to endure a great deal. Malnutrition and disease were facts of life. Food, clothing and shelter were no more than basic for most slaves. Field hands worked hard, for little or no reward. Physical and sexual abuse were common.

Most non-capital offences against slaves escaped punishment or censure and only a few whites were tried, convicted and sentenced for murdering slaves. As well as beatings and mutilation for persistent runaways, the most effective deterrent to slave resistance was the constant threat of being sold and separated from family and friends, since no state's law recognised the existence or validity of slave marriages.

# Slave Occupations

Slave occupations tended to be age-specific. Few able-bodied slaves aged fifteen to forty years of age were employed in occupations other than field work. Domestic servants tended to be older children, male and female, or older men and women no longer fit for heavy field work. Few slave owners could afford to have able-bodied slaves who specialised in a particular craft and worked full-time as carpenters or blacksmiths. Most urban slaves were female domestic servants, but some male slaves were employed as dock workers, craftsmen or factory workers employed in sugar processing or in sawmills.

Slaves were employed as house servants in the USA, as this eighteenth-century illustration shows. However, domestic service tended to be restricted to young slaves, or those too old or unfit to work in the fields.

# Plantation Labour

On those plantations employing fifteen or more slaves, slaves would work in gangs led by a driver chosen from among the male slaves on account of his strength, intelligence, loyalty to his master and leadership skills. The driver acted as an assistant to the owner or overseer, and personally supervised the work of his slave gang. Slaves employed in field work tended to be described as either plough hands or hoe hands. Plough hands were the fittest, able-bodied male and female slaves. Hoe hands were less fit, but were regarded as being more important than the members of the trash gang. This third group was made up of adults incapable of heavy field work and young children, and they were employed in tasks such as weeding and yard cleaning. The gang system in the American South was very similar to organisation of gang labour on plantations in the Caribbean and South America(see page 28).

# Domestic Life

Most slaves lived in wooden cabins or huts, and received a food allowance from their owners. It was common practice for field hands to receive four sets of clothes each year. Male field hands would be given trousers and a shirt, and women a dress. These clothes would have been sewn together by slave women, often using cloth that was specially manufactured in American textile

These log cabins were home to black field workers in Georgia, USA, in the 1860s.

mills to be sold to slave owners. Since boots and shoes seldom fitted properly, most field hands chose to work barefoot.

Many slaves were allowed to grow vegetables and keep chickens on small plots of land. Some were allowed to sell their produce at markets, or barter them for other goods. However, these garden plots were privileges that could be removed at the slave owner's discretion, and slaves were not able to pass on their property to their children or grandchildren.

## Urban Slavery

The number of slaves employed in the towns and cities of the South was not significant. In the years immediately before the outbreak of the Civil War in 1861, slaves made up less than ten per cent of the population of the largest cities in the slave-owning states, and no more than five per cent of the population in smaller towns. Most owners were wary of allowing their slaves to associate with urban slaves, or the free African Americans who tended to live in urban areas rather than in rural regions. One abolitionist noted that,

 *a city slave is almost a freeman, compared with a slave on a plantation.*

# Free African Americans

In the slave-owning states, most free African Americans lived in the upper South where more than ten per cent of all African Americans were free by 1810. Outside of that area, in the four decades before the outbreak of the Civil War, the number of free African Americans in the South decreased as states passed laws that made it very difficult for owners to free slaves. Free African Americans were encouraged to move north or west, despite the prejudice and discrimination they could face in those regions. In the northern states, freedmen, as they were known, were denied a vote and legal protection, and were threatened by racist gangs or mobs.

About 30 per cent of the free African Americans living in the Southern states were described by their neighbours as 'people of colour'. Some were the descendants of unions between French or Spanish slaves and their owners, while others were refugees from the French colony of Saint-Domingue. These free people were called 'mulattoes' in official census documents, but some preferred to call themselves by the less offensive name of 'Creoles', which was a name also used by the European descendants of French and Spanish colonists. Some African American Creoles owned slaves. Another group of free 'coloureds' consisted of those freed slaves who were the sons and daughters of slave owners, whose parents had chosen to distinguish between them and their other slaves. This was a custom that was common in South America, but was much less common in the United States of America.

# Christianity and Slavery

Some African captives were Christians before they arrived in the New World, but the widespread conversion of slaves to Christianity only began in the second half of the eighteenth century, and was accelerated by religious revivals among free Americans during the first half of the nineteenth century. In the last decades before emancipation, most slaves were Methodists or Baptists, like most of their Southern owners. In fact, a significant proportion of slaves attended the same services as their owners, although they worshipped in segregated slave galleries.

A religious revival in the USA at the beginning of the nineteenth century led to most slaves being converted to Christianity. This illustration from 1810 suggests that a slave's best hope of freedom would come from heaven ... 'their day of grace has begun to dawn!'

Free African Americans had formed their own 'African' Baptist or Methodist churches in the late eighteenth century. In 1787, the Free African Society had been formed in Philadelphia by former slaves. Richard Allen, a freed slave, had founded the Bethel Church, and this grew into the African Methodist Episcopal Church in 1816. African churches were opened in the cities of the North, and in some urban areas of the South. African American communities, finding themselves excluded from so many organisations by prejudice and discrimination, went on to set up schools and other associations to serve their own communities.

## Voodoo

At the same time, pre-Christian beliefs and practices persisted among rural slaves within their own families. Superstition, magic and folk remedies retained their hold on many illiterate farm labourers, and some slaves used potions, charms and rituals to ward off evil spirits, treat infections and frighten enemies. In southern Louisiana, the fusion of African beliefs and elements of Catholicism known as voodoo was popular, but it was virtually unknown in the rest of the South.

# The Movement Towards Abolition

For most of the eighteenth century, few Europeans questioned the nature of the slave trade between Africa and the European colonies in the Americas, but towards the end of the century, an increasing number of people began to demand the abolition of the trade. The first Europeans to openly campaign against the slave trade were the Quakers, or Society of Friends, who declared in 1761 that no person engaged in the slave trade could be a member of their religion.

A significant move against the slave trade in the United Kingdom was made by Granville Sharp. He tried to use existing laws to fight against the trade. His most dramatic success concerned a runaway slave called Thomas Lewis who had been kidnapped by his former owner, and put on a ship bound for the West Indies. Sharp obtained permission to bring Lewis back to London, and for his case to be heard in court. The result was that a British court had to admit that it was not clear whether or not it was legal to possess a slave in the British Isles. In 1772, the case of James Somersett came to court. He was a slave who had lived as a free man in London for two years before being recaptured by his former owner. Sharp hired a team of lawyers who persuaded the judge, Lord Mansfield, that Somersett was a free man, and that it was illegal to force a runaway slave to leave the British Isles.

Granville Sharp (1735–1813) restraining a sea captain from taking a slave to his ship in 1767. Sharp was a founder of the British Society for the Abolition of the Slave Trade. He concentrated on fighting test cases through British courts to establish legal precedents that would force the trade to come to an end.

# The *Zong*

In 1781, horrific events on the slave ship *Zong* focused public attention on the evils of the slave trade. The ship's captain was an experienced slave trader called Collingwood. He had mistaken Jamaica for Saint-Domingue, and after eleven weeks at sea, seven crew and over eighty slaves had died. In order to make a profit on the voyage, Collingwood ordered his crew to chain together and throw overboard more than 130 slaves so that he could make a claim to the ship's insurers. Ten slaves who witnessed what was happening committed suicide. Following a court case, the ship's owners were able to force the insurers to pay them £30 for each slave whom Collingwood had drowned.

# The Campaign Begins

The Society for the Abolition of the Slave Trade was founded in 1787. The Society decided that its main purpose should be to campaign for an end to the transatlantic slave trade. The Society decided that the abolition of slavery would be too expensive if slave owners had to be compensated for the loss of their slaves, and the effects of the abolition of slavery on the colonies and transatlantic trade would hit the British economy too hard. Instead, by abolishing the slave trade they would end the wars in Africa that were fought to enslave thousands of Africans each year, bring to an end the horrors of the Middle Passage, and force slave owners to treat their slaves better, since they would be more difficult to replace.

Leading British abolitionists who campaigned for an end to the slave trade between the British Empire and Africa included Sharp, Macaulay, Wilberforce, Buxton and Clarkson.

**39**

# Anti-Slave Trade Arguments

The Society claimed that sugar could be produced more cheaply in British-controlled India using free labour, or indentured servants, rather than by relying on slaves in the Americas. It argued that the transatlantic slave trade was holding back the development of British trade with India and the rest of Asia. The Society also produced evidence that hundreds of British seamen involved in the triangular trade died every year, and those who participated in the horrors of the Middle Passage were brutalised by the way that they were forced to treat their human cargoes. In 1798, a poet writing under the name 'Guineaman' described his experiences as a sailor on a slave ship with these words:

*But some of them were sulky slaves,*
*And would not take their meat;*
*So therefore we were forced, by threats*
*And blows, to make them eat.*

# Gathering Evidence

Thomas Clarkson had been involved in setting up the Society in 1787 with Granville Sharp. Clarkson set himself the task of collecting evidence that would win support for the abolition of the slave trade. Embarking on his investigations in London, he visited and studied slave ships in the capital, as well as Bristol and Liverpool. He collected artefacts such as manacles, thumbscrews and branding irons. Despite intimidation and threats from slave ship captains and owners, Clarkson interviewed over 20,000 sailors and collected a mountain of evidence about the horrific conditions aboard slave ships. Much of this evidence was published, including detailed diagrams showing how slaves were stowed aboard the slave ships. First-hand evidence about the evils of the slave trade came from Olaudah Equiano who had been kidnapped in Africa as a child, but had been able to buy his freedom in the Caribbean. He later wrote about his experiences in *The Interesting Life of Olaudah Equiano*.

Kidnapped as a boy in Africa, Olaudah Equiano bought his freedom, became a leading abolitionist, and wrote his autobiography. He insisted on using his African name, rather than the slave name, Gustavus Vassa, given to him by his first owner.

# William Wilberforce

William Wilberforce was a wealthy man whom John Newton, the former slave trader who had become a clergyman, had persuaded to join the Society for the Abolition of the Slave Trade. Wilberforce soon became its leader. In 1788, he wrote that:

*The main object I have in view is the prevention of all further exports of slaves from Africa.*

Supported by evidence gathered by abolitionists that graphically illustrated the suffering of captives on the Middle Passage, Wilberforce worked hard to persuade Parliament to make it illegal to participate in the slave trade. However, the slave traders and slave-owning plantation owners had too many friends and allies among Members of Parliament, and Wilberforce's arguments failed to win the support of a majority of MPs.

As a consequence, the Society and its supporters stepped up their campaign for the abolition of the slave trade, and the abolitionists published even more horrific accounts of what happened on the Middle Passage and on plantations in British colonies. The pottery manufacturer, Josiah Wedgwood, produced china goods decorated with the Society's seal to publicise its campaign and raise funds for the abolitionist movement.

William Wilberforce (1759–1833) was thirty years of age when he began to campaign against the evils of the slave trade. As a Member of Parliament, he was able to put forward his arguments to the British government for the next eighteen years!

# Slave Revolt in Saint-Domingue

Meanwhile, events in the Caribbean were taking a different turn. In 1789, the French people overthrew their king and in 1793 executed him. On the Caribbean island of Saint-Domingue, the slaves soon followed the revolutionary example of their French masters and, following a bloody revolt, they attempted to abolish plantation slavery. Saint-Domingue's slaves burned down plantations and slaughtered slave owners and their families. Ten thousand colonists fled to other colonies in the Caribbean and North America.

## Jean-Baptiste Belley

In 1791, when the French National Assembly had decided to extend the Revolution's Declaration of the Rights of Man to include freed slaves and their descendants, but not slaves, French colonists had forced the government to back down. Three years later, a former Haitian slave from Saint-Domingue called Jean-Baptiste Belley, who was a deputy to the National Convention in Paris, made an impassioned speech that pledged Haitian loyalty to the cause of Revolution, but asked the Convention to abolish slavery. The Convention decreed that,

*all men, without distinction of colour, domiciled in the colonies, are French citizens, and enjoy all the rights assured under the Constitution.*

Belley demonstrated that African captives and their descendants could produce leaders of quality who could match their European counterparts in terms of eloquence and political skill.

Jean-Baptiste Belley was a former slave from Saint-Domingue who spoke at the National Convention in Paris on behalf of those of African descent who lived in France's Caribbean colonies.

## A Growing Momentum

The liberation of Saint-Domingue (to be called Haiti) and the freeing of all its slaves had far-reaching consequences in the Americas and Europe. The slave revolutionaries forced the French revolutionaries to tackle the issues of racial equality and slave emancipation. The revolt removed France as a commercial rival to the British in the Caribbean, and contributed to the British decision to abolish their slave trade with Africa. Moreover, the example of the Haitians encouraged slave rebellions in other colonies. Later, the Haitians would provide assistance to General Simon Bolivar in his struggle against European colonisation in South America.

In 1791, a former slave called Francois-Dominique Toussaint Breda led the armed forces of the French colony of Saint-Domingue against British and Spanish invaders. Dropping the name Breda, he called himself 'L'Ouverture' (French for 'opening'), and in 1801 he declared that the colony was an independent state.

# The British Relent

Back in Britain, every year for nearly two decades, Wilberforce tried, but failed, to persuade the British Parliament to abolish the slave trade. But in 1807, both Houses of Parliament voted to pass a law abolishing the slave trade between Britain, Africa and all British colonies. British traders and ships could no longer participate in the transatlantic slave trade. In fact, the Royal Navy would try to prohibit other countries' ships from trading in slaves.

In all, 283 British Members of Parliament had voted for the abolition of the slave trade, and only sixteen voted against. Despite Wilberforce and his fellow abolitionists having fought against the slave trade for more than thirty years, in the end, political and economic circumstances persuaded their opponents to accept that abolition was in British interests.

The British naval victory at Trafalgar in 1805 had ended the threat from the French and Spanish navies, and the British wanted to take full advantage of their sea power. They could stop and search foreign vessels, using the pretext of halting the transatlantic slave trade, to deprive the French, Spanish, Portuguese and Dutch colonies, as well as the American states, of new batches of African captives. In the process, they were able to disrupt enemy trade. This took place at a time when British prosperity no longer relied on slave labour in the colonies since domestic industries had developed rapidly. British plantation owners in the Caribbean were also keen to make life difficult for their rivals by ending the trade.

British naval supremacy was confirmed at the Battle of Trafalgar, and paved the way for British efforts to bring the transatlantic slave trade to an end, from 1807.

# British Opposition to Abolition

There were many reasons why it had taken so long to persuade Britain's political leaders to abolish the transatlantic trade in African captives. One reason was that the slave trade had many powerful supporters. Plantation owners based in the Caribbean, the merchants who bought their produce, and the absentee plantation owners living in Britain, some of them Members of Parliament, were well organised as well as powerful. They had enough wealth to bribe other Members of Parliament to support them. They also had the support of King George III until he became too ill to influence government policy. Many influential people were prepared to believe that the abolitionists had exaggerated the number of occasions when slaves had been badly treated. They believed that the enterprise of slave-owning planters had helped to make Britain wealthy and prosperous.

# Wars Against France

Another factor that delayed the abolition of the slave trade was the French Revolutionary Wars. Britain had joined an alliance of countries that had gone to war against the new republican government of France. This conflict did not end until 1815, when Napoleon was defeated at the Battle of Waterloo. These wars made heavy financial demands on Britain, and most politicians believed that ending the slave trade would be too costly. It was also claimed that the transatlantic trade was an essential training ground for the Royal Navy that defended the British Isles from invasion.

Napoleon (1769–1821), Emperor of France, embarked on a series of wars of conquest against other European states. These wars had repercussions for European colonies in the Caribbean, as well as North and South America.

# The Effects of British Abolition in the USA

Agriculture in the American South relied on slave labour. Once the British began to bring the legal trade in African captives to an end, slave trading between states grew in scale and profitability. As plantation farming in the upper South declined in states such as Maryland, Virginia, North Carolina and South Carolina, demand for slaves grew in states where cotton plantations were making large profits. As the *Charleston Mercury* noted before the Civil War:

*Slaves are as much and as frequently articles of commerce as the sugar and molasses which they produce.*

Slave traders were everywhere in the South. Some companies had branch offices in towns and cities throughout the slave states. They advertised in newspapers, offering high prices for fit and healthy slaves, and visited farms and plantations to offer owners cash for slaves who would fetch good prices at auction. New Orleans was the largest slave-trading centre in the Deep South, handling slaves from the upper South being sold to the thriving cotton and sugar growing areas.

The internal slave trade within the USA led to untold suffering within the African American community. In the decades before the Civil War, as slave traders sought to maintain profit margins, it was common for families to be split up as individuals were sold to the highest bidder. It was not unusual for husbands to be sold separately from their wives, and for parents to be separated from their children. A former slave, Josiah Henson, described how as a young child:

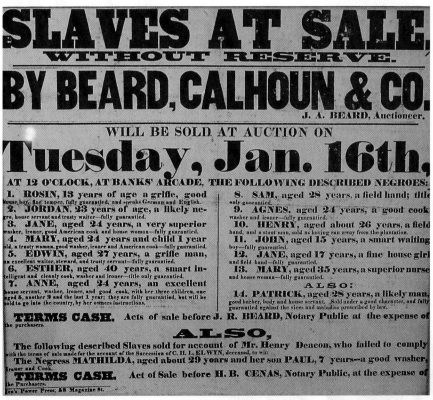 *My brothers and sisters were bid off first, one by one, while my mother, paralysed by grief, held me by the hand.*

The inhumanity of slave ownership and the trade in human beings is illustrated by this poster. It lists people for sale, giving their age, physical attributes, and details of any skills or training that will increase their value to a potential purchaser.

Poster image: SLAVES AT SALE WITHOUT RESERVE BY BEARD, CALHOUN & CO.

# THE ABOLITION OF SLAVERY IN THE USA

## Revolts and Sabotage

The most common form of resistance to slavery was called 'silent sabotage'. Many slaves expressed their discontent by vandalising owners' property, and stealing food and other objects from the masters and their families. Whenever possible, gangs of field hands opposed efforts to impose a strict routine on their working day. The result was that most gangs tended to work long hours at a leisurely pace, interrupted by short periods of intense activity, often carried out under the threat of the master's whip. Few field hands were forced to work on Sundays, and some owners felt obliged to pay their slaves to work on the Sabbath at harvest time.

The most extreme form of resistance to the institution of slavery in the South was confrontation. Slaves would offer physical resistance to whites in extreme circumstances, such as when they were provoked by violent or abusive slave owners or overseers, or threatened by the sale of a family member to another estate some distance away. The few major slave revolts that erupted were local affairs, and they were swiftly crushed by the use of armed force. The most bloody slave revolt in American history took place in 1811, when 500 slaves in Louisiana marched on New Orleans, led by a former slave-driver called Charles Deslondes. More than 60 slaves were killed in battle or executed in the aftermath of the rebellion. The most famous slave-led insurrection was Nat Turner's revolt in Southampton County, Virginia, in 1831. Turner held out for two months, until he was captured, tried and executed.

## Runaways

Most successful runaways were young adult males from the states of Maryland, Virginia, Kentucky and Missouri, fortunate in having less distance to travel to reach the free states in the North. Most fugitive slaves hid out close to their owners' plantations. Some eluded capture long enough to join the free African American

Many people risked their lives and freedom to assist runaway slaves to escape from their owners.

The fact that rewards were offered for the return of runaways suggests that people had to be encouraged to capture slaves who were fleeing from their masters.

population in the larger towns, but most runaways were captured.

Some runaways received food and shelter from sympathetic people whom they met on their journey, and others were guided by around 3,000 'conductors' on the so-called 'Underground Railroad' who broke the law to assist runaways. It has been estimated that possibly 75,000 slaves escaped to freedom using this network of routes north from the slave states. The fugitive slave, Harriet Tubman, is credited with having conducted at least 300 runaways to freedom, including escorting a group of eleven fugitives to freedom in Canada.

## Maroon Communities

A small number of escaped slaves formed groups of fugitives known as 'maroons' living in inaccessible swamps in Florida, remote sea islands in South Carolina, and unsettled areas of Georgia. Sometimes, the maroons would undertake expeditions to attack plantations and take slaves back with them to enlarge their communities. Persistent truants could expect to be brutally beaten or maimed, but even runaways who simply took off to visit friends or relatives, or escape censure for some minor misdemeanour, would be fortunate to receive no more than verbal abuse from their owners.

$00,00 REWARD!

RANAWAY from the subscriber, on the 10th inst., a Negro Man named Jack, about 35 years of age, about 5 feet 5 inches high, weighs 125 or 130 lbs., dark copper color, some teeth out before, has an impediment in his walk as if he were stiff in the hip joint, his clothing consisted of black cloth pantaloons, blue cloth close bodied coat, and black over coat, boots and over shoes—boots have been lately half-soled;—also a black oil cloth satchel. I will give $25 if taken in the county, or $100 if taken out of the State, or lodged in any jail that I may get him, or delivered to me in Haynesville, Clinton County, Missouri.
TAYLOR HULEN.

March 12, 1858.

# Early American Abolitionists

In the early years of the American republic, anti-slavery ideals were popular in Northern and Southern states. Many recognised the conflict between the ideals of the republic's constitution and the harsh realities of slave life. Slavery did not sit well with liberal, humanitarian beliefs, and many Americans had been influenced by the radical social and political ideas that came out of Revolutionary France. Other Americans recognised the conflict between slave ownership and Christian beliefs. This period saw a rapid and irreversible decline in the number of slaves in the Northern states.

By the early nineteenth century, the rapid economic development of Southern agriculture and the fact that plantation production exploited large numbers of slave labourers appeared to push anti-slavery organisations into the background. A key figure in reviving the anti-slavery movement was William Lloyd Garrison who founded the anti-slavery newspaper *The Liberator* in 1831. In 1833, the American Anti-Slavery Society was founded, demanding immediate emancipation without compensation to slave owners. Within a few years, membership of the Society's 1,500 branches was believed to stand at 250,000 in the Northern states.

The masthead of William Lloyd Garrison's abolitionist newspaper, *The Liberator*, 1831. This newspaper published stories of successful runaways and provided details of slave owners' abuses of their slaves.

Frederick Douglass, a runaway slave who became an agent for the Anti-Slavery Society, travelled widely in the North, lecturing against slavery and campaigning for the rights of free African Americans. He published the first of three autobiographies, *The Narrative of the Life of Frederick Douglass: An American Slave* in 1845. To escape recapture, he sailed to Britain, and in 1846 British friends purchased his freedom from Hugh Auld, his former owner.

Many people in the North were abolitionists because they believed that slavery was cruel and inhuman. Some opposed slavery because of the harm that it did to whites in slave-owning areas. They believed that it encouraged cruelty to other humans by brutalising owners and overseers, while poor whites who did not own land or slaves found it difficult to find work, and became lazy or turned to crime.

# Uncle Tom's Cabin

Harriet Beecher Stowe's novel appealed to hundreds of thousands of Americans in the free states who sympathised with the plight of the novel's African American hero.

In March 1852, Harriet Beecher Stowe published her novel, *Uncle Tom's Cabin*. She based this work on stories of runaway slaves, and set out to persuade her readers that the evils of slavery had to be ended immediately. Around 100,000 copies of the book were purchased in its first week of publication, and more than two million copies were bought within two years. Other anti-slavery novels had been published before, including Richard Hildreth's *The Slave, or the Memoirs of Archy Moore* in 1836, but *Uncle Tom's Cabin* tapped into a new mood. Mary Chesnut, the wife of a plantation owner, complained in her diary in 1862 that:

*People (in the North) expect more virtue from a plantation African than they can find in practice among themselves.*

# Emancipation Plans

This illustration, dating from 1852, shows one of the novel's characters, George, handing out certificates of freedom to his slaves. Note how the artist has chosen to portray the slaves' reaction to this news in a most undignified light.

Some Northerners feared the results of emancipating slaves while others opposed granting freed African Americans political equality. Consequently, some Northerners supported the idea of setting up colonies of former slaves in either Central America or West Africa, rather than encouraging former slaves to become citizens of the USA. Most Northerners opposed the spread of slavery into the Western territories, and this increased political tensions between free and slave states.

# Sectionalism

Southerners feared that the North would try to forbid slavery in the West, and both 'sections' became concerned at the possibility of a shift in the balance of power between North and South that would mean either the slave or free states would be in the majority. The Missouri Compromise of 1820 had balanced the number of slave-owning and free states, and this had limited discussion about the spread of slavery into the West for a generation.

The 1850 Compromise was supposed to solve the problem of allowing California to enter the Union by allowing it to become a free state, so long as stricter laws were passed to make it easier to return escaped slaves to their owners. The Kansas–Nebraska Act of 1854 tried to allow both states to join the Union, so long as both held a referendum to decide whether either would be a slave-owning or a free state. This attempt to find a compromise led to violence and bloodshed.

Tensions between free and slave states grew, and in 1857 the decision of the Supreme Court in the Dred Scott Case concerning the ownership of a runaway slave appeared to extend the rights of slave owners into the free states. In 1859, the abolitionist John Brown tried to initiate a slave revolt in Virginia, and the whole issue of slavery and states' rights went on to dominate the presidential election of the following year.

John Brown's attempt at a slave revolt ended in failure. Here, Union soldiers are bringing Brown's followers out of the engine house at Harpers Ferry.

CAUTION!!
COLORED PEOPLE
OF BOSTON, ONE & ALL,
You are hereby respectfully CAUTIONED and advised, to avoid conversing with the
Watchmen and Police Officers of Boston,
For since the recent ORDER OF THE MAYOR & ALDERMEN, they are empowered to act as
KIDNAPPERS
AND
Slave Catchers,
And they have already been actually employed in KIDNAPPING, CATCHING, AND KEEPING SLAVES. Therefore, if you value your LIBERTY, and the Welfare of the Fugitives among you, Shun them in every possible manner, as so many HOUNDS on the track of the most unfortunate of your race.
Keep a Sharp Look Out for KIDNAPPERS, and have TOP EYE open.
APRIL 24, 1851.

This poster of 1851 illustrates some of the national tensions. It warns fugitive slaves to stay away from watchmen and police officers in the Boston area who were acting as kidnappers and slave catchers.

# National Tensions

By 1860, national politics in the USA were sectional, and politicians and parties reflected the widening gap between North and South over the issue of slave-holding in the Western territories. Issues that resulted from territorial expansion and economic growth, such as the further development of the railroads, were viewed from the perspective of both sections. Increasingly, many Northerners believed that there was a slave power conspiracy that influenced the actions of the executive and decisions taken by the courts. Many Southerners were convinced that the institution of slavery could be preserved only by secession from the Union.

# Abraham Lincoln

When the Republican candidate, Abraham Lincoln, was elected President of the USA in 1860, many Southerners were convinced that he would try to abolish slavery. Starting with South Carolina, Southern states voted to secede from the Union. In March 1861, the Vice President of their newly-formed Confederacy said that,

*our Confederacy is founded upon ... the great truth that the black is not equal to the white man. That slavery, subordination to the superior race, is his natural and normal condition.*

Lincoln believed that slavery was morally wrong and against the spirit, if not the letter, of the Declaration of Independence and the other ideals of the Founding Fathers. He opposed the expansion of slavery into the Western territories, but he was not an abolitionist at that time. In 1861, he said,

*I have no purpose, directly or indirectly, to interfere with the institution of slavery.*

Following his election victory, Lincoln was not convinced that the secessionists in the South would carry out their threat to divide the Union, but he was careful not to say or do anything that would heighten the crisis.

Abraham Lincoln (1809–65), US President, 1860–65.

# The Civil War

Lincoln was not prepared to allow the Southern states to set up a separate Confederacy. The President's primary war aim would be to preserve the Union, not to abolish slavery. As late as August 1862, the President wrote,

*What I do about slavery, and the coloured race, I do because I believe it helps to save the Union ...*

The war aims of the Confederacy were to preserve slavery, and to fight a defensive war against invasion from the North. As the war progressed, the South hoped to force the North into negotiating a truce that would recognise Southern independence. To this end, the Confederates hoped to enlist support from the United Kingdom and France. To achieve these aims, the Confederates had to defeat the Union forces in the East, the West and at sea.

In the East, the fighting centred on Northern Virginia, the Shenandoah Valley, Maryland and Pennsylvania. In the West, the fighting took place in Tennessee, Georgia and along the Mississippi River. The war at sea focused on Union attempts to blockade Confederate ports and restrict Southern trade with other countries, and Confederate attempts to prevent the Union forces combining their military forces to capture ports and fortresses on important rivers. The first major battle of the war took place at Bull Run near Washington DC, in July 1861.

A contemporary illustration of the battle of Bull Run in July 1861. People in the Northern states took a keen interest in news of the campaigns and battles of the Civil War, often taking place hundreds of miles to the south and east.

# War and Freedom

From the beginning of the war, Lincoln's generals had to deal with those slaves freed by advancing Union forces. In 1861, General Butler, who commanded a Union army base in Virginia, declared that three fugitive slaves who had escaped from a Confederate labour battalion were enemy property liable to be seized, or 'contraband of war'. He gave them food, shelter and work and, within two months, there were about 1,000 contrabands at his base. Later in the same year, General Fremont, who commanded the Union forces in Missouri, issued a proclamation declaring that the slaves of every rebel in the state were free.

# Emancipation Proclamation

In September 1861, Lincoln modified Fremont's proclamation so that it freed only those slaves used directly in the Confederate war effort. However, it was not long before Lincoln recognised the strategic value of emancipating all slaves in enemy territory. In 1863, Lincoln's Emancipation Proclamation meant that the abolition of slavery had become one of his government's war aims. As commander in chief, the President declared that all slaves in rebel territory were,

*thenceforward, and forever free.*

The Proclamation did not free any slaves, since slaves living in the four slave states loyal to the Union, and in Confederate territory captured by the Union armies, were not included in the terms of the document. What the Proclamation made clear was that the North was fighting for a Union freed from the moral burden of slavery.

Emancipated slaves travelling north following Lincoln's proclamation in 1863. This fictional scene exaggerates the number of freed men and women who headed north from Confederate territory to the free states.

# On The Road to Emancipation

W. T. Sherman (1820–91), general of the Union army in Georgia and South Carolina, 1864–65, in heroic pose.

At the end of 1864, General Sherman issued Special Field Order Number 15, granting the Carolina Sea Islands and all of the fertile plantation land 48km inland, from Charleston to Jacksonville, to freed slaves. General Saxton who commanded the Union occupation forces settled more than 40,000 freed slaves on this land until Lincoln's successor, President Johnson, pardoned the rebel landowners and returned their property to them.

Despite the success of the Union campaign after 1863, most slaves were not emancipated until the Confederacy had been defeated. Although more than 500,000 contrabands escaped to freedom behind Union lines, more than three million slaves continued to work on Southern farms and plantations throughout the Civil War. The Confederate war department drafted thousands of slaves to work as labourers for the army, and many other slaves accompanied their masters to war as servants. However, many slaves gave food, shelter and other aid to Union prisoners of war trying to escape from Confederate custody. As well as working as free labourers, contrabands assisted Union troops by supplying them with local intelligence, and the absence of owners and overseers serving in the Confederate armed forces reduced the contribution of slave labour to the Southern economy.

In January 1865, the Thirteenth Amendment to the US Constitution was passed, abolishing slavery in every state of the Union, and emancipating nearly four million African Americans. Within four years, the Fourteenth and Fifteenth Amendments and the Civil Rights Act of 1866 confirmed the voting rights and civil rights of the freed slaves.

A Union victory parade held in Washington DC on 23 May 1865. The victorious North celebrated the defeat of the Confederacy, rather than the emancipation of the slaves.

# Reasons for Union Victory

The Union's superior economic resources contributed to the defeat of the Confederacy. Another factor was the collapse of the Confederate forces' supply system, and the subsequent weakening of Southern morale in the face of Union advances. This led to a flood of desertions from the Southern armies in the later stages of the war. In addition, President Lincoln had a firm grasp of strategy and knew that defeating the Confederate army was more important than occupying enemy territory. To achieve this end, he takes full credit for appointing Ulysses S. Grant to command his armies in 1864. In sharp contrast, Jefferson Davis as Confederate leader failed to convince the Southern people that he could lead them to victory.

# The Contribution of African Americans

The contribution of African Americans to the Union war effort had made possible the defeat of the Confederacy. Ten thousand African Americans served in the Union navy from the outbreak of the war. At the end of 1862, Lincoln authorised the enlistment of freed slaves into the Union army. More than 190,000 African Americans served in the Union armed forces. They made up nearly ten per cent of enlisted men, they received equal pay from 1864 onwards and, despite racial prejudice, nearly 100 African Americans were commissioned in the army. Seventeen African American soldiers and four sailors received Congressional Medals of Honour. The rebels did not authorise the enlistment of slaves into the Confederate army until March 1865, and they had surrendered before a regiment of slave troops could be established.

A proud soldier who had escaped from slavery to join the Union army. This illustration appeared in *Harper's Weekly* magazine in 1864.

# African American Culture

The ending of the legal slave trade with Africa and the rest of the New World led to a decline in the influence of African culture on American slaves after 1800. Instead, their shared, common experiences as enslaved rural labourers became important. The movement of slaves within the USA due to the domestic slave trade that developed when the slave trade with Africa ended, also helped to create a common culture among slaves in the South.

Elaborate slave marriage and funeral ceremonies were used to mark key stages in human existence. Slave children grew up listening to similar fables and folk tales told throughout the South. Great respect was accorded to the preachers, folk doctors, midwives, musicians and storytellers who served the African American slave community, and who helped to develop a distinct African American identity before the outbreak of the Civil War.

Measured in thousands rather than millions, some freed slaves marked their emancipation by moving west, constructing railroads, working on cattle ranches and claiming their own homesteads on the Great Plains. It was not until the twentieth century that millions of African Americans abandoned their rural traditions and headed north to live in an urban environment.

The defeat of the slave states in the Civil War opened the way for the westward expansion of the railroad network. Some African Americans took the opportunity to move west, but the main feature of this development was the destruction of the tribes who lived on the Great Plains.

# African American Abolitionists

In the decades before emancipation, some of the most effective spokespersons for the abolitionists were runaway or former slaves, such as Frederick Douglass, J. W. Loguen, Sojourner Truth, William W. Brown and Henry H. Garnet. In 1843, Garnet announced to the Convention of Free People of Colour, in New York:

*Remember that you are four millions! Let your motto be resistance, resistance, RESISTANCE!*

Sojourner Truth (c.1797–1883), a former slave who became a Christian preacher and abolitionist. Like so many African American abolitionists, her work was overlooked by historians until the second half of the twentieth century.

African American abolitionists wanted to shape their own destiny. They had no desire to be the beneficiaries of the paternalism of their abolitionist allies, such as William Lloyd Garrison and John Brown. Frederick Douglass tried, but failed, to persuade John Brown not to attempt his raid on Harpers Ferry in 1859.

Frederick Douglass (c.1818–95) became such a famous runaway abolitionist that a song was composed in his honour by Jesse Hutchinson in 1845.

# The Black Codes

In the American South, the original Black Codes had been introduced as early as 1680 to prevent slave rebellions, but these laws had been developed to control every aspect of slave life. Plantation owners, their overseers, their friends and relatives, as well as local townspeople and police, served in patrols set up to enforce the codes in their area. Plantation owners usually paid for the patrols, and failure to serve in one led to a fine. Each patrol was mounted on horseback, armed and accompanied by dogs, and headed by a captain. The patrols could seize and punish any slaves whom they considered to be absent from their plantations without permission, or guilty of breaking the local curfew for African Americans. Slaves who tried to resist the patrol could be shot, and patrols could enter slave cabins to search for weapons, or simply to intimidate the African American community. After emancipation, it was easy for racists to adopt the patrol model and use it as an effective method of shutting off African Americans from most avenues of freedom and self-expression.

THE FUGITIVE'S SONG,

FREDERICK DOUGLASS

A Graduate from the "PECULIAR INSTITUTION"

HIS BROTHERS IN BONDS.

FUGITIVES FROM SLAVERY

FREE STATES & CANADAS.

**57**

# THE EFFECTS OF ABOLITION ON AFRICA

## Seeking Alternatives

The British vessel, *HMS London*, chasing a slave trader's dhow, or yacht, near Zanzibar in East Africa. European states tried to bring the African slave trade to an end during the second half of the nineteenth century.

The long-standing trade in slaves across the Saharan region did not increase sufficiently to replace the export of slaves across the Atlantic. Attempts to preserve the transatlantic slave trade meant dealing with illegal traders who were often unable or unwilling to guarantee steady profits for African merchants. In comparison to the trade in captives, the total value of exports of palm oil, timber, gold and other products to Europe and the Americas was small. Some West African states had developed their own plantation agriculture, using slaves to produce rice, coffee and cotton. A significant success was the spread of peanut or groundnut cultivation for export, from the Senegal River region to Sierra Leone. Another positive development was the growth of the cocoa industry on the West African Gold Coast from the 1860s.

However, within forty years, small trading stations had become huge European colonies that incorporated former independent African states. Sierra Leone and Liberia became colonies for small communities of former slaves. Around 13,000 African Americans had settled in Liberia by 1867. By the end of the nineteenth century, the British colony of Sierra Leone controlled around 43,000 square kilometres of territory, and the British colony on the Gold Coast expanded to take control of the Ashanti Confederation and extensive 'Northern Territories'. Within forty years, the tiny British colony of Lagos had grown to include most of present-day Nigeria, the second largest state in Africa today. The West African colonies of other European states grew in a similar fashion during this period.

# European Paternalism in Africa

The modern map of Africa, with its regular boundaries drawn along lines of latitude and longitude, bears little or no relation to the boundaries of ancient kingdoms and empires. Instead, it is a product of nineteenth-century European aggression. Many Europeans perceived the failure of so many African economies to find alternatives to the slave trade as a clear sign that Africans were somehow less advanced than themselves. The long and brutal history of African servitude in the Americas had encouraged many Europeans to adopt a paternalistic attitude towards Africa that justified its subjugation and colonisation, so long as it was accompanied by the expansion of Christian missionary activities.

A map of Africa at the end of the nineteenth century, showing the imperial acquisitions of European states.

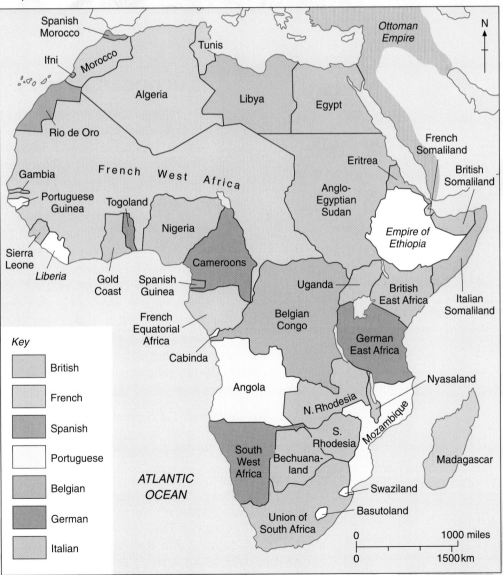

Key
- British
- French
- Spanish
- Portuguese
- Belgian
- German
- Italian

Spanish Morocco
Ifni
Morocco
Tunis
Ottoman Empire
N
Algeria
Libya
Egypt
Rio de Oro
French Somaliland
French West Africa
Eritrea
British Somaliland
Gambia
Anglo-Egyptian Sudan
Portuguese Guinea
Togoland
Nigeria
Sierra Leone
Liberia
Gold Coast
Spanish Guinea
Cameroons
Empire of Ethiopia
Uganda
British East Africa
Italian Somaliland
French Equatorial Africa
Belgian Congo
German East Africa
Cabinda
Nyasaland
Angola
N. Rhodesia
Mozambique
S. Rhodesia
South West Africa
Bechuana-land
Madagascar
Swaziland
ATLANTIC OCEAN
Basutoland
Union of South Africa
0          1000 miles
0          1500 km

# The 'Scramble for Africa'

This attack on Dahomey by French troops in 1892 involved the murder of a large number of Africans. Africans were no longer needed as captives, but those who survived these attacks were to become subjects of European states.

The destruction of independent African states in West Africa in the decades following the European withdrawal from the slave trade, was repeated in the European conquest of North, South and East Africa in the same period. African resistance provoked brutal reprisals to safeguard European colonists. In the second half of the nineteenth century, an Islamic revival in much of Africa provoked further European conquest.

Several European states expanded existing colonies, founded new colonies, or established protectorates where land was not occupied by the European state, but the territory was recognised as being in that state's sphere of influence.

## European Rivalry

In Europe, participation in what became known as the 'Scramble for Africa' was regarded as a defensive act. Europeans states believed that their African colonies had to be protected from economic competition from the colonies or protectorates of other European states, as well as attacks from local tribes and their rulers. At that time, there were intense political and economic rivalries between European states that made them keen to acquire new African colonies and extend existing colonies, often simply to prevent territory falling into the hands of rivals. One British politician wrote in 1892:

 *We are to effect the reconquest of Equatoria and occupy the Albert Lakes and the whole basin of the Upper Nile. Why? For fear of the French, the Germans, the Belgians etc, etc.*

Technological developments in nineteenth-century Europe meant that African armies could do little more than delay the advance of European armies into the interior of the continent. Europeans tried to temper this aggression by claiming that they were striving to wipe out African slavery, and Africa's slave trade with Asia.

# European Colonies in Africa

The British, long established in Cape Colony on the southern tip of Africa, extended their colonies in West Africa, seized territory in East Africa, gained control over Egypt, which had been under Ottoman Turkish rule, and with Egypt dominated Sudan. The French took over most of West and Equatorial Africa, and Madagascar in East Africa. The Portuguese established their control over Angola and Mozambique while Spain ruled the northern part of Morocco and the area of Western Sahara. Germany took territory in South-West Africa and East Africa, now known as Namibia and Tanzania, and Italy established colonies in what are now Libya, Eritrea and Somalia. An African poet in Ghana wrote in 1900:

*'We've come to trade!!' they said,*
*'To reform the beliefs of the people,*
*To halt oppression here below, and theft,*
*To clean up and overthrow corruption',*
*Not all of us grasped their motives,*
*So now we've become their inferiors.*

# Rubber Terror

King Leopold II of Belgium personally controlled the Congo Free State from 1885 to 1908, a vast territory that was bigger than the United Kingdom, France, Germany, Spain and Italy combined. In this protectorate, all suitable land was divided between concession companies. In rubber-growing areas, forced labour, hostage-taking, brutal beatings, chain gangs and the destruction of whole villages were employed to subdue and control the African population. These atrocities, committed in the name of the ruler of a small European state, highlight how far the balance of power in Africa had shifted in favour of European colonists.

Similar forced labour systems for extracting rubber were in place in the French territories west and north of the Congo River, in Portuguese-ruled Angola, and in German-controlled Cameroon. African refugees who fled across the Congo River to escape Leopold's ruthless regime often fled back to escape the French brutality in Congo-Brazzaville, and the population loss in this region was nearly 50 per cent within twenty years. The 'rubber terror' was one of the most barbaric episodes in the European colonisation of Africa.

Tippu Tib, a powerful African slave trader in the 1880s, grew very wealthy from the sale of captives and ivory to other traders. Tippu Tib's lands were conquered by a Belgian army, and made part of the Congo Free State.

The rule of Leopold II over his personal empire in Africa, was one of the most brutal and bloodthirsty episodes in the modern history of Africa.

# UP FROM SLAVERY

## American Reconstruction

When the American Civil War ended in 1865, around four million American slaves had been emancipated. For the next few years, national politics in the USA were dominated by discussions on the nature and extent of the reconstruction programme that would be directed at the former slave states. This was done without the leadership and guidance of Abraham Lincoln, who had been assassinated at the end of the war.

Legislation passed and ratified by Congress between 1865 and 1870 granted equal civil and political rights to all African Americans. The Civil Rights Act of 1866 defined all persons born in the United States as American citizens with equal rights. The Fourteenth Amendment to the constitution ratified in 1868 incorporated the Civil Rights Act's definition of citizenship into the constitution, and the Fifteenth Amendment ratified in 1870 declared that,

President Ulysses S. Grant (1822–85), signed the Fifteenth Amendment to the US constitution in March 1870. African Americans soon discovered that laws and constitutional amendments did not guarantee civil rights in a racist community.

*the right of citizens of the United States to vote shall not be denied or abridged by the United States or by any State on account of race, colour, or previous condition of servitude.*

However, in line with the views of most Americans, there would be no major social welfare programme to assist freed slaves. As the abolitionist Frederick Douglass had said in 1862,

*the best way to help them is just to let them help themselves.*

Instead, the Freedmen's Bureau was established in May 1865, to distribute food to refugees and the destitute of every race, provide limited health care, establish free labour farming, and assist in the establishment of schools for the children of former slaves. The Bureau's affairs were wound up in 1872.

## Sharecropping

Racial prejudices in the South forced the authorities to establish separate facilities for former slaves and their children, often providing inferior services to African Americans. Having freed the slaves without compensating their former owners, the federal government was not willing to go further and confiscate the owners' plantations and redistribute the land to former slaves. However, governments in the South sought to establish a free labour economy, and former slaves celebrated their freedom by refusing to work for overseers or under the gang labour system. As a result, the plantation system of production soon disappeared. Many female former slaves marked their freedom by abandoning fieldwork, and many families opted for rental or sharecropping agreements (see below) rather than wage labour. The dream of owning their own land was achieved by some since about twenty per cent of African American families in the former slave states owned their own farms by the end of the nineteenth century.

The Shore family – African American homesteaders in Nebraska, 1887. Behind them are the sod houses in which they lived.

This image of an African American farmstead presents an idealised vision of life in the rural South after the Civil War. In material terms, life did not improve for most freed African Americans for many decades.

Sharecropping became more common in the South in the 1870s. Croppers of any race paid landowners a share of their crop in return for the right to work the land. They used the rest to feed themselves and buy the tools, equipment, seeds and livestock they needed. In the words of one former slave, sharecropping was more attractive than wage labour since,

*I am not working for wages, but am part owner of the crop ...*

However, for most freed labourers employed in agriculture, whether or not they were sharecroppers, life remained hard.

# Buffalo Soldiers

After the Civil War, African American soldiers who wanted to continue in military service were able to join one of four segregated units either in the Cavalry or Infantry. These units were stationed in the West, where they protected migrants and homesteaders, safeguarded passenger and freight transport, hunted down outlaws and participated in campaigns against Native Americans, who called them 'Buffalo soldiers'. During the Spanish-American War, African American troops served with distinction in Cuba and the Philippines.

# Jim Crow

The fifty years before the First World War were made more difficult for most African Americans by racist violence and intimidation. The federal government did not act on their behalf as many were prevented from exercising their right to vote. 'Jim Crow' segregation laws were introduced to block the path to full citizenship for most African Americans in the South. These laws and rules segregated African Americans from the rest of American society in many states, and denied many their most basic civil rights. Both the National Association for the Advancement of Coloured People (NAACP) and the National Urban League (NUL) were founded in this period, to campaign for civil rights and demand that the republic provide,

*freedom and justice to all.*

Booker T. Washington (1856–1915), was born a slave, but became a teacher and went on to establish his own school, then college, for African Americans at Tuskegee, Alabama.

# The Great Migration

By the beginning of the twentieth century, the majority of African Americans were literate and many had received degrees from institutions of higher learning. A few, like Booker T. Washington and W. E. B. DuBois had emerged as national figures in their work to achieve access to education, and full political and civil rights for other African Americans. African American artistic genius in music, painting, sculpture, literature and dance was recognised in the USA and Europe. This period also marked the beginning of the Great Migration of African Americans from the rural South to the urban, industrial North in the search for new opportunities.

# Marcus Garvey

The Jamaican Marcus Garvey and his Universal Negro Improvement Association (UNIA) represented a crucial phase in the African Americans' struggle for justice and equality. Garvey arrived in the USA at a time of African American discontent, marked by race riots and racial tension, and he became leader of the largest movement in African American history. The UNIA incorporated the Black Star shipping line in 1919, to transport passengers between America, the Caribbean and Africa, and to serve as a symbol of African American pride and prestige. In 1922, the federal government indicted Garvey on fraud charges – he was imprisoned, and then deported to Jamaica in 1927.

Marcus Garvey (1887–1940) drives through the streets of Harlem, New York, in a plumed hat and uniform. Garvey was a huge icon for many African Americans.

# Civil Rights

The stuggle for justice was reignited in the 1950s, when Rosa Parks and other African Americans refused to give up their seats on segregated buses in Montgomery, Alabama. They sparked off a campaign against the laws that denied African Americans their full civil rights and forced them to use separate but not equal facilities. One of the civil rights campaign's leaders was a preacher called Martin Luther King, Jr. who declared that:

Martin Luther King (1929–68), seen here front row, far left, leading a vast crowd at a civil rights rally, 1963.

*We have no alternative but to protest.*

The African American boycott of Montgomery's buses led to their desegregation, and this was a significant step towards achieving equality for African Americans in the Deep South. Restaurants and other public places were soon desegregated, and in the 1960s, President John F. Kennedy pushed for African American students to be taught in desegregated public schools. His successor, President Lyndon B. Johnson, supported new legislation aimed at restoring full equal rights to African Americans, including the right to vote in state and federal elections.

# Emancipation and Inequality in the Caribbean

Apart from freedom, emancipation brought few other benefits to freed slaves in most Spanish, Portuguese, French, Danish and Dutch colonies in South America and the Caribbean. There was no redistribution of land that would have prevented freed slaves, who had little or no education and few transferable skills, from sinking to the lower ranks of the society. Economic power rested in the hands of former slave owners. Political power was shared by a small elite that consisted of those who boasted of their European ancestry, and those with a mixed race background that distanced them from the most disadvantaged freed slaves.

## Saint-Domingue

The exception was the French colony of Saint-Domingue, where the leaders of a successful slave revolt had declared Saint-Domingue to be an independent republic under its alternative name of Haiti, in 1804. When Dessalines, the republic's founder died two years later, the state was divided between a former soldier called Petion, and a former slave who had bought his freedom, Henri Christophe. Between them, these men and their followers created a unique society in the Caribbean. Most slave owners and their families had fled or been killed. The ruling elite consisted of the descendants of liaisons between African slaves and their owners, the extended families of slaves who had been freed before the revolts, and those former slaves who had acted as leaders of the slave revolts between 1791 and 1804, and had been rewarded with promotion and positions of power and influence.

## A Melting Pot

Following the abolition of slavery, developments in the labour market further complicated the racial composition of former colonies in South America and the Caribbean. Contract or indentured labour immigration led to large Asian populations from India and Indonesia being established in Suriname, Guyana and Trinidad, and smaller populations being settled in Jamaica and a number of other British Caribbean islands. Large-scale immigration from Spain during the first half of the twentieth century further marginalised the

These houses in Port of Spain on the Caribbean island of Trinidad remind us that for many of the descendants of the region's slave labourers, poor housing, poverty, crime and low life expectancy are facts of life.

African Caribbeans on islands such as Cuba, Puerto Rico and the Dominican Republic. Post-emancipation society in most former colonies was stratified by race and ethnic background, with former slaves and their descendants, and the surviving remnants of the region's indigenous peoples, invariably the victims of every form of discrimination and racial prejudice.

# George William Gordon

A demonstration by former slaves in 1865 outside the courthouse in Morant Bay, Jamaica.

In the British colony of Jamaica, George William Gordon, the son of a plantation owner and a slave mother, had urged fellow freed slaves to protest at their lack of education and employment opportunities, in peaceful and non-violent ways. In 1865, the British put down a rising of former slaves and their families, and the Governor announced that he held Gordon responsible for the trouble, although he had not taken part in the rising. Gordon was tried for treason and hanged. It was clear that the world's leading imperial power was not prepared to listen to appeals for racial equality made by some of their Caribbean subjects. Society in British Caribbbean colonies was to remain hierarchical and authoritarian for decades, based on ethnic and racial origins inherited from slave times.

# MODERN SLAVERY

## Angola

Since the abolition of chattel slavery in the Americas, the term 'slavery' has been used to refer to a wide variety of human rights violations and slavery-like practices throughout the world. In many places, including Africa, forced labour or debt bondage became the modern forms of slavery that continue to blight millions of lives today.

At the beginning of the twentieth century, in the huge Portuguese colony of Angola in West Africa, a system of voluntary contracts for paid labour allowed Portuguese traders, known as labour agents, to bargain with local chiefs. In exchange for guns, ammunition, rum and other goods, the chiefs would ensure that men, women and children were handed over to plantation owners to be employed as forced labour. Henry W. Nevinson published details of this trade in 1906, and pointed out that for colonists,

*the only motive for slavery is money-making, and the only argument in favour of it is that it pays.*

In 1961, there was a rebellion against the system of forced labour, followed by a Portuguese campaign of terror that led to the deaths of at least 20,000 Africans. Guerrilla warfare against Portuguese rule lasted for more than twenty years until Portugal granted the colony its independence in 1975. However, various forms of forced labour or bondage exist in Africa and throughout the rest of the world today, despite legal efforts at national and international levels to abolish these practices.

Angolan rebels undergoing attack training for guerilla warfare, 1961.

## Totalitarian States

Over the past 100 years, totalitarian regimes have not hesitated to use slave labour. In the USSR, Stalin used millions of political

The Nazis forced tens of thousands of their victims to work as forced or slave labour, such as these inmates of Dachau, one of the earliest concentration camps, established in 1933.

prisoners as slave labour on huge construction projects, making the captives in labour camps a key factor in his economic plans. The use of forced or 'corrective' labour declined after the dictator's death, but it continued to exist in various forms until the collapse of the Soviet Union in 1991. During the Second World War, the Nazi regime employed hundreds of thousands of Soviet prisoners of war, the inmates of labour camps, and conscripted labour from occupied Western Europe as slave labour in factories, mines and farms. According to the historian, Milton Meltzer, by 1944, there were more than seven million slaves working for the Nazis, who were,

 *degraded, beaten and starved, and often left to die for lack of food, clothing and shelter.*

In China, Mao's 'reform through labour' programme forced victims of the communist regime into labour reform camps in order to work on major construction projects and produce cheap consumer goods for export.

# Modern Slavery

The United Nations defines slavery as the condition of someone over whom any or all of the powers attached to the right of ownership are exercised. Member states are bound to eradicate chattel slavery, serfdom, debt bondage, the exploitation of children, servile forms of marriage, forced labour and every form of sexual slavery. African nations whose populations were depleted by the slave trade have considered asking for compensation for centuries of exploitation and forced labour inflicted by European states and their former colonies.

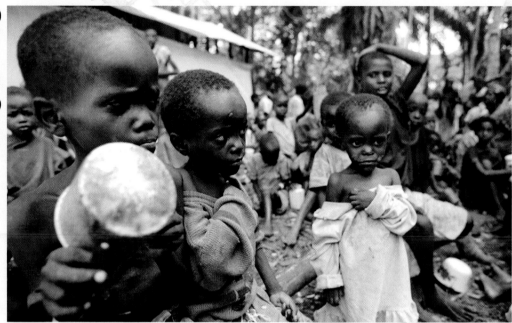

Poverty-stricken children wait for food in a refugee camp. Throughout the world, hundreds of thousands of people have become refugees to escape the horrors of civil war.

## Poverty

Evidence from the International Labour Organisation, human and civil rights groups and other investigations confirms that slavery and slavery-like practices can still be found in the world today. A common factor linking most forms of forced labour or servitude is the extreme poverty endured by so many people, whether they are agricultural labourers displaced by debt, war or climate change, or refugees fleeing political or ethnic conflict or natural disaster. Parents are often involved in slave traffic, abandoning or selling their children to traders. They hope that their sons and daughters will be employed as domestic servants or learn a useful trade, but are aware that they could become young victims of the sex industry.

## Child Slavery

Despite laws passed against child slavery in many states, it has been reported that millions of children are employed as slave or forced labour in factories and workshops in the Indian subcontinent. Children as young as six or seven can be forced to work for fourteen hours per day in textile factories. They are frequently beaten, and are too terrified of what might happen to them if they run away from the employer who paid their parents for their bonded labour. In South America, forest clearance and other environmentally-destructive enterprises often use debt bondage to obtain labour. Impoverished rural workers are allowed to run up debts to pay for their transport to the remote forests where they have been promised work. Their wages are held back to pay for debts owed to the company for equipment, accommodation and food.

Throughout the world, modern lightweight weapons have enabled children to be used in combat as child soldiers. Many more children have been used by armed forces as spies, messengers, servants and prostitutes. Some children have been kidnapped and recruited forcibly into armies and guerrilla groups, but others have been driven into the military by poverty and abuse at the hands of employers and occupying forces. Some governments and armed groups use children because they believe that they are easier to condition, with or without the use of alcohol and drugs, into unthinking obedience. Most child soldiers are aged between fourteen and eighteen, but many are recruited from the age of ten or even younger. Girls and boys are at risk of rape, sexual harassment and abuse.

Boys training as guerrillas at a secret base in Eritrea represent the modern face of slavery for many children. These boys would have had little or no say in their adoption by the soldiers who control their lives, and who could order them to their deaths in battle.

## Global Economics

Pressure groups have expressed concern at what they regard as the abuse of power by the world's leading nations, and the growing poverty in many nations, as governments, multinational companies and world bodies appeared to globalise capital and economic development. Campaigners have tried to encourage consumers to boycott goods produced by forced or bonded labour, and turn concern into action against exploitative labour practices and their consequences for the health and welfare of their victims.

Distance and primitive communications allowed eighteenth-century consumers to ignore the horrors of slavery and the slave trade. Consumers in the twenty-first century, however, have knowledge about the horrors of modern slavery at their fingertips, due to the revolution in communications technology that has taken place since the 1970s.

# Who Bears the Blame?

David Livingstone (1813–73) worked as a child in a Scottish textile mill, and went on to become a Christian missionary who campaigned against the horrors of the African slave trade in the second half of the nineteenth century.

In the nineteenth century, Christian missionaries and explorers, such as David Livingstone, wrote accounts of their expeditions into the African interior and raised public awareness in Europe and North America of the atrocities committed by slave traders. These missionaries, confident of their moral superiority over Africans, worked to abolish slavery and the slave trade, and reshape African society to the European model, by supporting the colonisation of Africa.

At the beginning of the twenty-first century, a number of South American, Caribbean and African states called for the United Nations to declare colonialism and slavery to be crimes against humanity. They also demanded reparations, or compensation, for the long-term effects that slavery and colonialism have had on so many regions. They accused the United States and many European countries of being largely responsible for the poverty and racial tensions that have blighted so many lives.

In response, some former colonial powers claimed that the horrors of slavery and the slave trade were not region-specific. They used as evidence the long-established slave trade between Africa and Asia. States opposed to the demand for reparations suggested that they would be prepared to acknowledge a moral obligation to those countries that suffered from slavery and colonisation. Several former colonial powers said that some, but not all, aspects of colonialism had been damaging. This suggests that there is still some way to go before paternalistic attitudes towards Africa and South America are extinguished in some parts of Europe and North America.

# GLOSSARY

**abolitionists** supporters of various campaigns to end the slave trade, or slavery, when the legal slave trade had been abolished

**bills of exchange** bills that traders received for slaves, which could be exchanged for cargoes of plantation produce that would fetch high prices in Europe

**Black Codes** laws originally introduced to prevent slave rebellions, but by the time of American independence had developed to control every aspect of slave life

**colony** an area of land that another country controls, and often settles in, with or without the full co-operation of the area's original population

**Confederacy** the Confederate States of America, set up by the states that seceded from the United States in the 1860s, but defeated in 1865

**contrabands** slaves living in territory captured by Union forces, or runaway slaves who reached Union forces during the American Civil War; war contraband was any enemy property that was captured by military action

**dysentery** a disease causing severe diarrhoea that often killed African captives on the Middle Passage, due to the effects of dehydration

**emancipation** the setting free of slaves

**Enlightenment** eighteenth-century intellectual movement that believed that rational, critical study and analysis should be applied in all matters

**feudal rights** a medieval landlord's right to service in the form of work, goods or other duties

**gang system** a system of field labour on large plantations in which gangs of slaves perform various tasks according to their age, fitness and skills

**guerrilla** irregular, often ill-trained soldiers who use ambush and hit-and-run tactics against better-trained, more powerful opponents

**indentured servants** servants who signed a contract that bound them to work for a master for a set number of years in return for food and shelter, and possibly training or transportation to a colony

**Indian territory** the vast area of North America, west of the Mississippi River, that would be settled by millions of migrants in the fifty years after the American Civil War; most of the tribes that inhabited this land would be attacked, defeated and consigned to their own limited territory or reservations by the last decade of the nineteenth century

**Jim Crow** a term to describe the vast number of laws, rules and regulations that segregated African Americans from other Americans in the years following the American Civil War, up to the 1960s

**maroons** freed slaves and runaways in remote regions of the Americas who maintained their independence from the slave-owning communities close to where they lived

**Middle Passage** the journey undertaken by African captives to the Americas by ship

**plantation** a large area of land on which a single crop, such as sugar, tobacco or cotton, is grown

**reconstruction** the programme of aid directed at the defeated Confederacy at the end of the American Civil War, in the hope that the former slave states could be restored quickly to full membership of the Union

**republic** government without a monarchy, but by an appointed or elected head of state

**sectionalism** the division of communities or political life along rigid lines based on a single issue that forces groups to ignore what they have in common with each other

**serfdom** a medieval form of forced labour, where farm labourers and their families worked for a landowner, had few legal rights, and were not allowed to leave their place of work without the permission of the landowner

**sharecropping** a form of agriculture in which tenant farmers promised a share of their next crop to their landowner in return for credit to purchase seeds, tools and other resources

**slave-driver** an assistant to a slave owner or overseer, who supervised the work of a slave gang; often, the driver was a trusted slave who received privileges for performing this role

**slave overseer** an assistant to the slave owner who supervised the work of the slave-drivers and the slaves

**smallpox** an infectious disease that was common in Europe until the nineteenth century, and caused the deaths of millions throughout the world until it was eradicated in the second half of the twentieth century

**staple** one of the main or usual crops grown in a particular area

**trading factories** fortified settlements where European merchants traded with local merchants and traders, guarded by European and local troops

**transportation** a form of punishment by which convicted criminals are used as forced labour in a colony or settlement for a set number of years

**Underground Railroad** an informal network of more than 3,000 sympathetic people who broke the law by assisting slaves escape to freedom in the Northern states, or Canada

# TIMELINE OF EVENTS

| | |
|---|---|
| 1492 | Christopher Columbus made landfall in what would become known as the Caribbean or West Indies |
| 1500 | Portugal took possession of Brazil |
| 1655 | Jamaican slaves formed first large maroon community |
| 1761 | Society of Friends banned people engaged in the slave trade from membership |
| 1772 | British ruling against forcing a runaway slave to leave UK |
| 1787 | Free African Society formed, USA; Society for the Abolition of the Slave Trade founded, UK |
| 1791 | Extension of French Declaration of the Rights of Man to include freed slaves and their descendants, but not slaves; slave revolt in Saint-Domingue |
| 1794 | Slavery abolished in all French colonies |
| 1802 | Napoleon I restored slavery in all French colonies |
| 1804 | Saint-Domingue declared independence |
| 1807 | British ended slave trade within British Empire |
| 1815 | Most leading European states affirmed their opposition to the slave trade |
| 1820 | Missouri Compromise, USA |
| 1831 | Nat Turner's slave revolt, USA |
| 1833 | American Anti-Slavery Society founded |
| 1834 | Slavery abolished throughout British Empire |
| 1848 | All slaves freed in the French and Danish colonies |
| 1854 | Kansas–Nebraska Act, USA |
| 1857 | Dred Scott Case, USA |
| 1859 | John Brown's attempt at slave revolt in Virginia, USA |
| 1861 | American Civil War began |
| 1863 | Emancipation Proclamation, USA |
| 1865 | American Civil War ended; Thirteenth Amendment to the US Constitution; British put down a rising of former slaves in Jamaica |
| 1866 | Civil Rights Act, USA |
| 1885 | King Leopold II of Belgium took personal control of the Congo Free State; Europe's major powers agreed guidelines for the further colonisation of Africa |
| 1886 | Slavery in Spain's colonies ended |
| 1888 | Slavery abolished in Brazil |
| 1890 | Seventeen major powers agreed to put an end to African slavery |
| 1944 | Seven million Nazi slaves employed in Europe |
| 1945 | United Nations established |
| 1950s | Labour reform camps in China; American civil rights campaigns |
| 1961 | Rebellion against forced labour in Angola |
| 1964 | Martin Luther King, Jr. awarded Nobel Peace Prize |
| 1975 | Angolan independence |
| 1991 | USSR collapsed, ending forced labour |

# FURTHER INFORMATION

Of the thousands of books about the transatlantic slave trade, slavery in the Americas and its abolition, and the aftermath of abolition in the nineteenth and twentieth centuries for the Americas and Africa, the following are among the best starting points:

James Walvin, *A Short History of Slavery*, Penguin, London, 2007
Hugh Thomas, *The Slave Trade*: *History of the Atlantic Slave Trade, 1440 – 1870*, Phoenix, London, 2006
S. Drescher and S. L. Engerman, *A Historical Guide to World Slavery*, Oxford University Press, Oxford, 1998
David Eltis, *Economic Growth and the Ending of the Transatlantic Slave Trade*, Oxford University Press, Oxford, 1987
Peter Kolchin, *American Slavery*, Penguin, London, 1995
James M. McPherson, *Battle Cry of Freedom: the Civil War Era*, Penguin, London, 1990
Milton Meltzer, *Slavery, A World History*, Da Capo Press, New York, 1993

There are many interesting and useful websites that contain reliable information on the slave trade and related topics.
www.spartacus.schoolnet.co.uk/USAslavery.htm
amistad.mysticseaport.org
www.loc.gov
www.princeton.edu
www.antislavery.org
http://slavetrade.parliament.uk/slavetrade/index.html
www.direct.gov.uk/en/slavery/index.htm

# INDEX

Page numbers in *italics* indicate pictures.